D1302012

"This book is a detailed g   jing the divine
opportunities that are arc   ring message
backed with real-life stori\

"This incredible book is a treasure trove of practical ideas for making the most out of every opportunity that God presents in your conversations with others. Don't miss out on this amazing message from Ryan Montague."

"*Divine Opportunity* will completely flip your view and perspective of your day-to-day 'passing' moments in life. You will never view opportunities for 'small-talk' the same way again once you fully realize what God can do even in seemingly 'meaningless' moments of life."

"Truth be told, most of us find the idea of 'evangelism' to be an intimidating assignment—even those of us who know full well it is a scriptural mandate. I love Ryan Montague's approach in *Divine Opportunity* because it puts sharing faith within everyone's reach ... it helps us 'put the cookies on the bottom shelf,' which is exactly as Jesus would have it. His stories are a terrific inspiration as well!"

"We all strive to be just as efficient and technically proficient as our surroundings, but the resulting isolation and independence leave a void and flatness to life and work. Dr. Montague gently points us to everyday moments in which the true meaning of our lives is found. With small but intentional shifts in our disposition, we may suddenly discover the fullness of everyday life in relationship with others and God. *Divine Opportunity* is not a prescription for success but rather an adjustment of perspective that allows us to see the fullness of everyday life as a connected path to wonder and personal growth."

"In our social media driven world our face-to-face relationships and the conversations they produce are quickly becoming a lost art. Fortunately, Dr. Montague helps us think about how invested God is, and therefore, how intentional we should be about those whom we live our lives beside."

— **Dr. Gary Black, Jr.**

Author of *Preparing for Heaven* and *The Theology of Dallas Willard*

"*Divine Opportunity* is a captivating collection of stories about people being open and obedient to God's word...which is sometimes loud and clear and at others, unique and mysterious. The assignments given at the end of each chapter offer open-ended questions and activities perfect for a growth group or family study! *Divine Opportunity* inspires and excites me to be ready and aware of God's plan for my life filled with the chances to serve, honor, and obey!"

— **Debi Gutierrez**

Peabody award-winning television host, keynote speaker, and comedian

"This inspiring, engaging, and practical book leads us all to deeper relationships with God and others."

— **Quentin J. Schultze, PhD**

Author of *An Essential Guide to Interpersonal Communication*

"Ryan Montague does something amazing in this book. He attempts to do what God has called us all to do, which is to make something sacred out of the mundane. Ryan's contention is that we can make seemingly insignificant encounters into something profoundly divine. Allow this amazing thought leader to guide you into not only a different way of looking at chance encounter but into a truly unique way of living your life."

— **Eric L. Wilson**

Spiritual director and author of *Faith: The First Seven Lessons*

"Twitter, Snapchat, Facebook, and Instagram, all of which are making email feel like a 20th century relic, are transforming inter*personal* communication into inter*functional* communication. In *Divine Opportunity* Ryan Montague brilliantly restores hope and focus on the important Kingdom principle that God created humanity to be in relationship with Him and with others. *Divine Opportunity* is a beautiful reminder that drawing closer to God will draw us closer to each other."

— **Edgar D. Barron, EdD**

Former Vice President of Communications and Creative Services at Promise Keepers

Chair, Leadership and Organizational Psychology, Azusa Pacific University

"Wow! Spiritually mature wisdom brought to life with stories of innocent discovery; *Divine Opportunity* is a 'must read.' Rich in emotional and social intelligence, it will be life changing for many. In a world swept up in the latest high tech devices, discover the personal emotional triggers that will reveal your own divine opportunities. Written by a gifted Christian storyteller, *Divine Opportunity* will make you smile, cry, laugh and wonder at the same time. And, after all, isn't that what life is all about—finding ways to communicate with each other? Divinely inspired and masterfully done!"

— **Richard Brundage**
President, Center for Advanced Media Studies

"I'm a firm believer that God does some of his greatest work through relationships and most of that work comes through ordinary conversations. Ryan gives us real-life examples of God doing his greatest work. He not only shows us how to recognize them when they're happening, but to anticipate them as people who want to be used by God in building up the body of Christ. If you want to know how God can use you in the ordinary rhythm of life, read this book!"

— **Chris Lewis**
Lead pastor, Foothill Church

"Ryan Montague has called us to intentional, embodied connections with anyone in our daily lives. And then he gives us purposeful evidence that our lives can be filled with the extraordinary in the ordinary when we participate in divine opportunities available to all. Wonderfully inspirational and challenging!"

— **Dr. Dick Pritchard**
Professor emeritus and associate director
Azusa Pacific University Center for Vocational Ministry

"Dr. Montague's book couldn't be more perfectly timed for this day and age of technological distractions and diminishing 'real time' encounters with people. For anyone desiring to be more effectively used by God to reach out and minister to others, this is your 'go-to' guide for spiritually grounded and extremely practical principles for the journey. It's loaded with real-life stories that are sure to encourage, inspire, and affirm those divine opportunities."

— **Jerry Kitchel**
Career mission worker and communication specialist

"Singing praises for *Divine Opportunity* and Dr. Ryan Montague! He has given us a much-needed report card on the state of affairs in the area of human connection along with practical tools and biblical truths to turn things around! As a worship pastor, I've found *Divine Opportunity* to be an encouraging and impactful resource as I co-labor with God and my fellow leaders to build His church!"

— **Larry Walker**
Worship pastor, Redeemed Life Church

"This is not a book you pick up and read in a day, but it is one that you have to take with you on a journey, reading a little each day. It pushes you beyond your comfort zone in every way possible. Memorable and emotional."

— Sofia Figueroa
Up and Coming World Changer

"Dr. Montague presents us with a personalized view into the world of godly relationships. Ryan observes that each of us should see people daily and should take the *Divine Opportunity* to say hello and listen to a story or two and be open to whom God would direct us if we were not constrained by time or technology. You have got to read this!"

— Bill W. Hughes
Author of *Escape from Anger: Step by Step*

What Readers Are Saying

"This reading has made me feel more convicted than any other book or article that I have read in the past. From this reading, I felt as though God was nudging me to realize how present He was in my past, and how active He wants to be in my future."

— Stephanie Escobedo

"I never thought that divine appointments were something for me. I felt too average and not special enough to either 'hear' God speak to me, or be influenced by the Holy Spirit to act. This reading just encourages me to go out, listen to what I feel I'm being 'told' and really connect with the Holy Spirit in a unique way."

— Jenn Koch

"As soon as I began the reading, I felt deeply convicted of shutting people out of my life. I challenged myself this week to start up conversations with those I would otherwise avoid or pass by. I also challenged myself to listen to God more often for divine prompts in connecting with others, especially strangers."

— Paige Penner

"This has been an extremely big problem for me lately, and I actually broke down about this tonight to one of my friends. I legitimately have so many things on my plate that I have forgotten what it means to slow down and share in small moments with people."

— Sarah Steuer

"I am encouraged from this reading to put down my phone, laptop, ear buds, and talk to people. How exciting and terrifying in the same moment. I am moved to look new people in the eye and greet them as if I am greeting Jesus himself. If I seek only God, I could be missing half of what life has to offer. If I seek only people that I am comfortable with, how shallow and boring will life be?"

— Matt Ross

"This reading is an in-your-face reminder that every day we have opportunities to be on the look-out for these moments God might put in front of us."

— James Dearborn

"This reading convicted me hardcore! I need to start putting more effort into being OK with uncomfortable meetings and conversations."

— Kjersten Jensen

"Many sections of this reading really spoke to me and made me realize that my relationships with others are far more important than other mundane tasks that I have on a daily basis. I have recently noticed that I have been putting many things in front of my closest relationships, and reading this section makes me want to change that."

— **Tai Carter**

"This reading definitely caused me to think about the way that I interact with others. It got me thinking about how many missed opportunities I've let go by, and has definitely convicted me to leave myself open to more opportunities. However, not all experiences have been missed! I've had my fair share of divine appointments that afterwards have caused me to step back and realize that it wasn't a well-timed coincidence, but was a 'God thing.'"

— **Dori Eisenthal**

"I can recall more than a few occasions where I walked away from a situation feeling down because I knew that I had an opportunity to step out and be intentional with people, even random strangers. I'm not sure why it is so hard to take that step in those situations – Pride? Fear? Whatever it is, I can't stand the feeling afterward. I am going to try to be more attentive to what is laid out in front of me, and if I feel that little nudge from God, I'm going to act."

— **Collin Parker**

"It challenged me to keep my faith, and believe in God's hand orchestrating every aspect of my day. I love the idea of divine appointments. I will continually pray for God's eyes, and believe that each day can be full of His opportunities."

— **Haley Jessup**

"Divine appointments and missed opportunities are concepts I was previously familiar with. Not because someone had to tell me but because I myself have felt that deep divine urge to talk to someone and have been obedient and disobedient at opposing occasions. This reading made me realize that divine appointments are not only important to God, but they're important to my personal growth."

— **Rachael Kemp**

"I absolutely loved the idea of having a manna jar. I never thought of something so crafty, yet something that could be filled with meaning and beautiful stories. I think that the manna jar is also a beautiful idea be-cause it reminds us of what we should be grateful for."

— **Camille Endacott**

DIVINE

— OPPORTUNITY —

DIVINE
— OPPORTUNITY —

FINDING GOD IN THE CONVERSATIONS
OF EVERYDAY LIFE

RYAN MONTAGUE, PhD

Divine Opportunity

Copyright © 2016 by Ryan R. Montague

Published in the United States by Credo House Publishers,
a division of Credo Communications, LLC, Grand Rapids, Michigan
www.credohousepublishers.com

ISBN: 978-1-625860-49-1

Cover art direction by Bistro Studios
Interior design by Nicolas Mulder
Proofreading by Chloe Stegman

Printed in the United States of America

First edition

Dedication

This book is dedicated to the Montague and Watson families! This book would not have been possible without all your love, support, encouragement, and guidance over the years. The joining of our two families was truly a divine appointment. It's the differing strengths of both our families that have come together and made this book what it is—an inspiring, motivating, and practical message!

To my wife, Debbie, thank you for your tireless support! You are the ultimate encourager—while also keeping things real. Your self-sacrifices have made this book possible. Many lives will be changed because of your sacrificial attitude, gracious love, and humorous encouragement. You are God's greatest blessing on my life.

To my kids, David and Makenna, may your lives be filled with divine opportunities. I pray that God blesses you with a manna jar that overflows with answered prayers and divine experiences.

Finally, this book is dedicated to all those who are seeking, searching, and longing for more in this crazy, mixed up, busy life here on earth. I pray this book will transform your daily walk with God and with others.

Contents

Foreword

This book became a very personal spiritual formation message for me. I have known and enjoyed my friendship with Ryan Montague for several years. We had talked about the content of his book on several occasions. And yet, as I read the pages of *Divine Opportunity,* I began to crave a deeper desire to look for God in the common everyday experiences of life. The principles and stories in this book are not only inspirational, they will help you become more and more aware of God's presence in places where perhaps, like me, you weren't looking for Him. After reading this book, I began a habit at night of asking a simple question, "Where was God's presence with me in today's experiences?" Wow! I began to see His hand in a simple conversation, or even a text from a friend. All of us can be helped so very much by just remembering God's working in our life at all times and even in the small stuff.

I have two hopes for you as you read through this book. One is that you will have a similar personal experience as I did, and meet God in a fresh new way. Someone once said, "If the Devil can't make you bad, he will make you busy." I find that sometimes we are just so distracted with our breathless pace of life that we miss the many encounters and opportunities that we can have with our Creator and Savior. It was Eugene Peterson in his paraphrase of Romans 9:27–33 describing people like you and me: "They were so absorbed in their 'God projects' that they missed God and went sprawling."

My second hope is that you will become more aware of the many incredible opportunities God gives you to share His love with others on a daily basis. Most of the time it's not in grandiose ways, but in small ways: encouraging a friend or a family member; or sending a text to someone you didn't even know was hurting. Just today, I listened to the small voice inside of my soul and called a special friend of mine. I honestly believed the Holy Spirit had prompted me to call. I didn't tell my friend that but just said, "You have really been on my mind. How are you doing?" With a longer pause than usual, my friend, who is a ministry leader, spoke with his voice cracking, saying, "My wife was just diagnosed with cancer. The timing of your call is incredible." Maybe I should have told him that this was a "divine opportunity" for me. But I just said, "You have been on my mind," and prayed with him over the phone. If God is the Creator and sustainer of life, then He can and does speak to our hearts and minds on a daily basis, if we listen. I think God will use the message of this book to heighten your awareness of His work and His love in and through your life.

Since this is Ryan's first book, and I'm guessing there will be many more books by him, let me say a few words about Ryan in closing. He is the real deal. He is fun and funny. He is a wonderful husband to his wife, Deb, and one of the more outstanding fathers I've ever seen to his beautiful children. He lives out what he writes about and he is a man of integrity. As a professor at Azusa Pacific University, Ryan is a favorite. He is a wonderful communicator but he also touches the lives of his students in deep and meaningful ways. Many of the students he works with tell me he is their favorite professor. He is relevant and a wonderful listener. As I read this book, I realized that this *Divine Opportunity* message is so much more about the life that Ryan lives out daily touching the lives of so many people. Ryan is a mentor to others and through these pages I think he will guide you to a deeper walk with God, like he did me.

Jim Burns, PhD
Dana Point, California

Introduction

A Prayer for the Reader

*For God does speak—now one way, now another—
though man may not perceive it. —Job 33:14*

In the name of the Father, the Son, and the Holy Spirit. Dear heavenly Father, we come before You, as writer and reader, to pray that You speak to us in and through this book. We come before You humbled with our hearts open, longing for Your words of wisdom and Your revealing grace. We pray that Your Spirit prepares our hearts and minds to recognize Your calling and Your ways as we work through each chapter. You and You alone hold the keys to the kingdom of eternal truth. We ask that You allow our hearts to be one so that the message and intent of each chapter is read and understood from the same life-giving outlook from which it was written.

Lord, we know that You speak to us in a multitude of ways, and we pray that You open our eyes, ears, and hearts so that we recognize Your calling. And, more importantly, we pray that You give us the courage to respond to that calling. We ask that You would prepare our hearts so that we are open to the challenges that each chapter may bring, and that You reveal opportunities for us to respond to those challenges in relationships with others around us.

We pray for this in the name of Your Son and our Lord and Savior, Jesus Christ. And all God's people said, "Amen."

For additional spiritual preparation, I encourage you to listen to the free song download "Speak to Me" and focus on the message of the song and connection it may have for you personally as you read through this book. You may even find it helpful to listen to the song before reading each chapter as a way to slow down, focus, and hear from God. You can download "Speak to Me" for free at: www.foothillchurch.net/speaktome

Chapter 1

Open Your Eyes to the Things Unseen

Put Down Your Armor and Open Your Heart

What is the first thing that comes to mind when you think of the word *armor*? Take a moment and picture a person wearing armor. Most people probably envision a medieval person standing tall, covered in metal armor with a shield and a sword, or perhaps a soldier in camouflage with a helmet, backpack, and rifle. For me, when I hear the word *armor*, I think of college students—college students walking to and from class wearing large sunglasses, carrying a cell phone in one hand and a drink in the other, with a thin white cable running from their cell phone to their ears. This is the modern-day form of armor. The only thing these students are missing is a pair of nose plugs and they will have successfully blocked the majority of their senses with relational armor.

Armor can be defined as any defensive covering. In a similar fashion, I use the term "relational armor" to refer to any defensive covering that restricts us from engaging in meaningful conversation with others. In the example above, this would include all forms of nonverbal cues and armored apparel: head down, expressionless face, cell phone in hand, ear buds in ears, and sunglasses covering one's eyes. With the addition of each piece of relational armor it makes it that much less likely that people even attempt to penetrate our social shield.

If you're anything like me, then your relational armor is less about the sunglasses, cell phone, and ear buds. Instead, your relational armor is your to-do list and the events scheduled on your calendar. Personally, I've used my to-do list to ward off more conversations and relationship-building opportunities than anything else. As friends, family, colleagues, and acquaintances come at me with suggestions to meet up, hang out, or go out to eat, I quickly bust out my to-do list and deflect all oncoming invitations as though each one is a sharply thrown ninja star. Unfortunately, my to-do list has become this invincible force field that keeps others at bay. I have to regularly confront myself with the question: am I really willing to sacrifice loving and caring for people in conversation in order to accomplish thirty more minutes of work?

In today's society, many people (myself included) walk through the city streets, hallways at work, and walkways of school campuses protected by all sorts of relational armor. That protection could be a tech-shield or a to-do list shield; either way, our defenses are up. In the last several decades, there has been an increase in individualistic and superficially-connected experiences.[1] It's ironic, but true—we live in a society that tricks us into being socially distant from people in close physical proximity yet superficially connected through technology to people far away.

Just think about the last time you stood in line at the bank, grocery store, or a coffee shop. How many people interacted with one another while standing in line? On the other hand, how many people interact (or at least pretend to interact) with people via cyberspace—through e-mailing, texting, or checking social media? This is an example of what I call "so close yet so far away" interactions. Have you ever had someone accidently bump into you because they were engrossed with their cell phone and totally unaware of the rest of the world? People can be located so near one another yet feel worlds apart in the social sense. On the other end of the spectrum, people can be so far apart physically yet feel "connected" socially. I use the quotation marks to highlight my slight skepticism of that connection.

There is an undeniable trend of devaluing and decreasing meaningful conversation in society today. A wary news reporter suggested that perhaps people should participate in "less tweeting, more meeting."[2] After all, it's the good old-fashioned, meaningful conversation that provides people with the greatest improvement to their well-being and increased happiness.[3] Don't get me wrong, e-mails, texts, instant messages, tweets, snaps, and Facebook updates certainly have their place in relationship building. It's just that the meaningful connections through those mediums are fewer and farther between. Ultimately, communication scholars, sociologists, and psychologists agree: it is not the *quantity* of the interactions that matter, but rather the *quality* of such interactions.

I should clarify a bit here. I am not as anti-cell phone, texting, and tweeting as I may sound at the start. These forms of communication can be beneficial when used in moderation. However, we Americans do not exactly excel in moderation. We do excel, however, in justifying our behavior. As my pastor recently stated, "We are masters of self-deception." And our justifications and self-deception lead us in the direction of overusing our cell phones and tablets. We rationalize and eventually trick ourselves into exchanging high *quality* interactions for high *quantities* of interaction.

Conversations Sparked by God

We live in a society that tends to isolate us from strangers in the name of keeping us connected. It seems more socially acceptable to ignore opportunities for face-to-face conversation than to embrace those opportunities. Instead, we retreat behind our relational armor as we passively interact with social media. Relationship experts at The Gottman Institute have gone as far as to say, "'Technology' invites us to avoid intimacy and we gladly accept the invitation."[4] Just recently, I was speaking with a group of college students who were opening up and admitting to wearing headphones, which weren't even playing music, in order to avoid conversation with others. Some even admitted to pretending to text in order to avoid interactions. And other students faked phone calls to dodge casual social exchanges.

Our society's ever-growing acceptance of face-to-face social avoidance raises an important question: what sparks and sustains the impulse or desire for people to engage others in conversation? It is my belief that the influence and guidance of God can spark the impulse and sustain people's desire to be in conversation with others. In my case, as well as in the case of many other Christians, it's the prompting, nudging, and sometimes convicting presence of God in our lives that does this. It is His influence and guidance that drives us to lay down our gadgets, put away our to-do lists, and initiate conversation with others. One of God's pastimes is creating divine opportunities for conversation and relationship building. Even in the direst situations and unlikeliest of circumstances, God can bring two people together to share something profoundly mutual, motivating, and transformational. This means we must keep our eyes, ears, and hearts open to the gift of opportunity God is blessing us with.

Knowing that God is about relationship building is all the more reason for us to pocket our cell phones and shed our relational armor. Instead, we should use our downtime to focus on God's will and motivation for the moment. Perhaps there is someone right next to you with whom God wants you to connect. Rather than listening to music, playing games, or checking status updates, try this: say a quick prayer and ask God to provide you with a divine opportunity to speak to that person. Do not underestimate what God can do in a conversation while waiting in line for your burrito, or on a thirty-minute phone call to your great-aunt at her nursing home while you drive home from work. Each of these conversations and all the other possibilities in between are occasions for divine opportunities, and ultimately spiritual influence.

These types of divine opportunities have the potential to result in meaningful connection with others. I refer to the fulfilled divine appointments as *divine opportunities* and the unfulfilled opportunities as *missed opportunities* for divine appointments. Here is the difference.

Divine opportunities are conversations in which you recognized God's role in bringing you together with another person. You or the other person recognized that the two of you had a meaningful conversation—not by chance, but because of God's guidance. There is an awareness that God helped you have a profound conversation, a conversation that could have come together only with God's help. This awareness might occur in the moment, or it may take place later as you look back on the conversation.

Missed opportunities, on the other hand, are those moments in which God urged or nudged you to start a conversation with someone, but for whatever reason you did not actually follow through. Missed opportunities may also come about in the midst of a conversation where God urged or nudged you to ask a particular question or make a particular comment, but the moment passed by. You might become aware of that missed opportunity in the moment itself, or you may recognize it only after the fact as you reflect back on the conversation.

Both divine opportunities *and* missed opportunities are life experiences that merit your deepest level of thought and consideration. If you have not previously given this subject your full attention, I urge you to make this a priority. God has wonderful, amazing, faith-building experiences in store for you, and the thought of anyone missing out on what God has planned for their lives is an absolute tragedy.

As one of my favorite philosophers, Martin Buber, once stated, "The meaning for the creation of life is to find God in and through engagement with others."[5] Isn't that a beautiful thought? This idea of engaging God in and through our conversation with others is difficult to keep in mind amidst the day-to-day busy living that engulfs us. But if we truly believe that all human beings are created by God as well as in His image, then we are indeed capable of engaging God in and through our engagement with others. And if we truly believe this, then it should certainly change the way we relate to people every day of our lives.

Self-Confession

I was at Starbucks trying to edit and revise this chapter, which is all about encouraging and challenging people to put aside their distractions, strike up meaningful conversations, and prioritize others' needs over our own to-do lists and agendas. As I worked on this chapter, I grew more and more convicted that I often don't even take my own advice when it comes to caring for others in conversation and relationship and putting people above my tasks and to-dos.

This prompting led me to shut down my computer, pack up my bag, go outside, and introduce myself to a woman I had seen inside Starbucks earlier. I had suspected that she might be homeless, and she was. Her name was Joy, and she was fifty years old; but because of a hard lifestyle, she looked much older (I, of course, didn't tell her that to her face, just in case you were wondering).

I'll be honest with you: this was not a smooth, easy-flowing conversation; it was all over the map. As Joy rambled, I sat and listened and asked questions. She opened the conversation by asking if I was a writer. Before I could even answer, she proceeded to tell me that she really wanted to write a horror story so that she could tell her stories about how badly people treat one another. This began to make more sense as she continued to talk with me that day.

Joy told me about the disconnection she had from her four children. At this point, she didn't even know where they lived. She was an alcoholic and a chain smoker—she smoked four cigarettes during our hour-long conversation and confessed she could drink thirty beers in an evening. She said that her lifestyle had torn up her insides, causing all sorts of health complications, and doctors had told her she doesn't have too much longer to live. Joy shared with me stories about how she had been beaten up by both men and women—they had punched her in the face, hit her over the head, and stolen what little money she had.

As she continued to share her story with me, Joy told me that both animals and people had peed on her while she was sleeping in nearby neighborhoods. She told story after story about how people had mistreated and abused her. She shared how both her parents had passed away, and that she missed them desperately. As I tried to comfort her that perhaps she would see them again one day in heaven, she replied, "Most people tell me the only place I'm going is hell."

Joy often skipped around to stories about run-ins with the police for loitering, receiving tickets for peeing in public, and driving under the influence. I don't think I heard one positive story in over an hour of talking with her. Needless to say, I didn't quite know how to respond to any of it, so I just sat and listened and tried to empathize with Joy. But to be frank, I couldn't even begin to understand what it would be like to experience anything she mentioned. I thought about how the only differences between Joy and myself were the family I had been born into, and the different people we had encountered throughout our lives. I thought about how easy it is for me to thank God for all the blessings I have received, and how hard it must be for her to thank God for anything.

The sad part is that there was really no way for me to help Joy, other than to sit and listen and let her know that someone cared enough to shake her hand, look her in the eyes, and ask her name. When our conversation came to a close, I asked if I could pray for her, and she seemed open to the idea. She took the last drag of her cigarette, put it out with her fingers, set it aside, and held out her hands for prayer. So I set aside my coffee (which is my own form of addiction), took her hands in mine, and prayed for her. Before I prayed, though, I tried to assure her that it doesn't matter what other people say about her, nor what she has done in her past. What matters is that God loves her. If she repents and asks God to forgive her of her wrongdoings, and truly believes in Jesus Christ, then despite what other people say about her, she will be reunited with her parents and Jesus in heaven.

I can't say that Joy seemed deeply moved by any of this. She didn't break down on the spot and call out for God. We just said our goodbyes and went our separate ways. I was probably more moved and impacted by it all than she was. In fact, what I prayed would be a divine opportunity for her was likely a divine opportunity for me. It was again a reminder that regardless of the petty things going on in my life or what I think I have to complain about, my troubles are nothing in comparison to what this woman had experienced in the past, what she is currently going through, and what she will still have to endure in the years to come.

Rather than spending so much time in self-pity or grumbling about the relatively minor difficulties I endure, I learned I ought to thank God that I have not had to go through any of the trials and difficulties that Joy had in her lifetime. In reflecting upon this whole experience, it became clear that this connection with Joy and this personal realization for myself would not have been possible had I stayed hunkered down behind my computer screen, my silver-apple wall of protection, and continued on with my work.

The Main Purpose

The main purpose of this book is to reveal that when it comes to divine opportunities, "There are no gifted or ungifted here, only those who give themselves and those who withhold themselves."[6] It is easy for Christians to hear stories of divine opportunities and to think that those types of experiences are only for pastors, missionaries, and modern-day prophets. This book is a simple reminder that divine opportunities are for *every* believer. It doesn't matter if you're "anointed by the Holy Spirit" or just coming to faith; it doesn't matter if you're a Baptist or a Catholic; and it doesn't matter if you're an introvert or an extrovert. What does matter is whether you allow yourself to recognize the opportunities all around you, and whether or not you subsequently commit yourself to exploring what God has in store for that moment.

Wholeheartedly, I believe you were meant to read this book. The fact that this book has found its way into your hands is a divine opportunity in and of itself. I pray that you have the courage to stay the course and not just consume these divine opportunity stories, but go out and experience them for yourself.

For some Christians, the divine connection between themselves, other humans, and God has already struck a chord and resonated in their relational lives. I cannot wait to share the collection of stories and experiences I have discovered during my research on divine opportunities.

The following chapters are filled with beautiful examples of how Christians are living out their faith, despite being faced with fears and relational barriers that might otherwise have kept them from engaging in such opportunities. This book can keep us all accountable—calling us to reflect upon the gift of opportunity set before us day in and day out. It is a direct challenge for all of us to get rid of our relational armor, keep our heads up and eyes open to the needs of others, and launch out in courageous obedience to God's promptings.

If you were to set this book down right now and go up and introduce yourself to someone new and they quickly shut down the conversation, do not feel defeated. In fact, there may be more people who reject your conversational invitations than accept them. I will admit that the weekend before I had my conversation with Joy, I tried walking across the room and introducing myself to a visitor after our church service ended. I thought I was going to meet someone new and get acquainted through a great conversation. But after I introduced myself, the guy simply shook my hand, said his name, and replied, "Nice to meet you." Then he turned abruptly and walked away, even as I was starting to ask him a question. It was a pretty humbling rejection. So if your attempts go absolutely nowhere, don't be discouraged. Keep your head up, and keep looking out for future opportunities.

Not the Main Purpose

This book is NOT meant to be a comprehensive theological argument for what is and what is not a divine opportunity, divine appointment, or missed opportunity. I am simply a Christian Social Scientist; I am not a theologian or a pastor. I realize that God is far bigger and far greater than I could ever hope to comprehend or put into words. I could never fully or completely describe and analyze divine appointments; those moments will always have an element of mystery about them that is incomprehensible. At the end of the day, I am a PhD professor of interpersonal communication and my goal is simply to provide you with some insights, challenges, motivation, and practical tools that can enable you to recognize and engage in more divine appointments and miss fewer opportunities.

This book, *Divine Opportunity*, is not meant to suggest that sometimes God is present and other times He is not. God is always present, always active, always moving. However, there are certain moments where God uses our thoughts, words, and actions to create turning points in our lives or the lives of others. These turning points come in both subtle and significant times in our lives, and it would be a shame not to take a closer look so that we can all expand our view, understanding, and awareness of such moments.

Discussion Questions

1. Which form of relational armor do you struggle with the most—technology armor or to-do list armor? What is one step you could take this week to purposefully put that armor down in order to make yourself more available to others in conversation?
2. How has the increase in technology impacted your relationships for better and for worse?
3. What is one divine opportunity you have experienced in the past?
4. What is one missed opportunity you have experienced in the past?

Chapter 2

Filling Your Manna Jar

*Do not forget to entertain strangers,
for by so doing some people
have entertained angels without knowing it.*

—Hebrews 13:2

A Divine Opportunity

The following divine opportunity story comes from my father-in-law, David Watson, a professor and chair of pastoral ministries at North Central University in Minneapolis, Minnesota. At the time of the divine opportunity, David was lead pastor at Central Assembly in Springfield, Missouri. He writes:

> As a pastor of a church in Springfield, Missouri, I had a pretty full plate that included church-wide meetings, staff meetings, individual member meetings, the responsibility of writing sermons, taking care of administrative duties, community outreach, and many other obligations—in addition to being a husband and a father. Needless to say, time was of the essence.

My story picks up one afternoon when I was between meetings and driving across town. As I began my drive between these appointments, a sudden feeling came over me that I was to go to the local hospital to pray for someone. However, I knew how much I still needed to get done that day and how short of a time frame I had between my scheduled meetings. But still, the Lord was speaking to me. I could not get this thought out of my head. As I contemplated the choice between getting to my meeting on time and being obedient to God's prompting, I ultimately committed to driving to the hospital to see if there was anyone to pray with, and, if not, then I would quickly turn around and get to the meeting.

Upon arriving at the hospital, I parked my car and quickly rushed inside. I walked in and checked with the woman working at the reception desk, with whom I was familiar from previous prayer visitations. She informed me that another pastor from our church had already been in to pray with people from our congregation. As I was having that conversation with the woman at the front desk, I noticed a man sitting off to the side reading a newspaper. He lowered his newspaper, set it aside, and quickly walked over to greet me.

As it turned out, this man was a janitor at the hospital. His job, primarily, was to clean up the hallways and patients' rooms. Earlier that morning, he had been cleaning a patient's room just after she had been diagnosed with a terminal illness. The woman just happened to have the TV on, which was tuned to a local morning broadcast. Prior to going to a commercial break, the broadcast transitioned to a pastor who was delivering a daily devotional and motivational word to the audience. Upon watching this, the woman, who did not go to church, turned her head up to the ceiling and said aloud, "God, if You really exist and You are really a God who cares about me, I want You to send that pastor to my room today to pray with me."

"Well," said the janitor, "after hearing this woman pray to God to send this pastor to pray for her, I told God that after my shift got over this morning at ten that I'd wait around for two extra hours until noon just to see if He would send this specific pastor to this particular hospital, and if He did then I would do my part. When you walked in at eleven fifty, right as I was about to leave, I heard your voice as you talked with the receptionist, and I recognized your voice from the TV program. I set down my newspaper, looked over, and sure enough, God sent you, the very pastor from the TV program, to this exact hospital. I would like to take you to pray for the woman. Would you come with me?"

Upon hearing this from the janitor, I knew that it was God's will. The feelings that I had while driving between meetings were confirmed as God's divine prompting. This was indeed a divine opportunity. I thanked the janitor for his assistance and I knocked on the door to the woman's room. When I walked into the room the first thing she said was, "It's you! It's really you! How did you know?" I told her that God had heard her prayer, that He cares about her, and He directed me to her to pray for her. I will never forget that moment when she realized how much God cared for her.

I love that story. I have heard David share this divine opportunity and many others from the pulpit. People's reactions are quite mixed when he shares it—some cry, some shout "Amen," and others even give the Lord a "clap offering." Almost everyone, however, is blown away by the impossible made possible by God in these moments.

However, when I hear these kinds of accounts shared with a large congregation, my fear is that people will believe the stories but discount the possibility of such mind-blowing divine opportunities occurring in their own lives. Christians might hear David sharing his divine opportunities, and then simply write off the idea that they are just as capable of experiencing these God-ordained moments in their interactions and relationships. If you were to meet David, you would realize just how passionate, faithful, and determined he is to do God's will, how outgoing and charismatic he is with others, and how people naturally gravitate toward him. When all of that is put together and we compare ourselves to someone like David, it is easy to discount the possibility of such moments happening for the likes of us.

That is why I want you to reflect upon the divine opportunity described above and view this experience not from David's perspective but instead from the perspective of the janitor. After all, "there are no gifted or ungifted here, only those who give themselves and those who withhold themselves,"[7] and that goes for everyone—including both pastors and janitors.

On that particular day, the janitor was sensitive to his surroundings and the people whom God placed in his path. The janitor made the decision to give himself over to the Lord, stick around long after his shift ended, and patiently and obediently wait for the arrival of this unknown pastor.

The janitor should be our model for divine opportunity behavior for us as everyday Christians.

From my observations, we live in an "apathetically-sympathetic" society. We are capable and willing to sympathize with people, just as long as we don't have to do much about it. Think about the last time you heard of someone in need. Perhaps you uttered the phrase, "I'll be praying for you." How long did that last? Maybe one prayer? Consider the janitor in this situation. He could have found out about the patient's health situation and diagnosis, overheard her prayer, and sympathized without action. Had the janitor been apathetically-sympathetic, David would have arrived at the hospital, marched in to greet the receptionist, asked if anyone needed prayer, and would have, essentially, been turned away. He would have walked right out and headed on to his meeting.

Another alternate ending could have looked like this. The janitor, while cleaning the woman's room, could have been wearing headphones and listening to music. Off in his own little cleaning world, he would have completely missed out on hearing the woman's prayer because he was busy switching out the trash can liners while humming along to Michael Jackson's "Man in the Mirror." As a result, no one would have been around the reception area to escort David to that patient's room because the janitor would have left when his shift ended. By the time David arrived, the janitor would probably be at home watching reruns of *Fresh Prince of Bel Air* with his feet kicked up, completely oblivious to the divine opportunity of which he could have been a major part.

Ultimately, it's people who are open, aware, and actively pursuing God—like the janitor—who have inspired me during the course of my interviews and daily discussions with people about divine opportunities. These are the actively-empathetic Christians to whom I turn as examples for what is possible in my own life.

Don't Forget About the Small Things You Can Do for the Lord

David's hospital story raises another point of concern. I fear that when hearing divine opportunity stories, many people may lose sight of the small things they can do for the Lord. Keep in mind that divine opportunities are not always going to seem miraculous or astonishing. Many divine opportunities are "small yet significant."

Upon a quick reading of David, the janitor, and the hospital patient's divine opportunity, it might seem easy to view that as one of those big, miraculous, and astonishing acts of God in and through people. However, if you'll humor me in yet another re-envisioning of what led up to the moment at the hospital that day—we might reveal still another perspective.

Let's rewind again to consider the janitor's actions. His part may have seemed small and relatively easy. It involved being aware of his surroundings; in particular, he was aware of the people who were a part of his work routine. He was simply paying attention to the people around him as he went about his daily duties. He obediently followed the intuitive prompting from God, and then he kept a watchful eye and stayed ready to respond when the opportunity arose. As a result, the janitor's "small" acts of listening, obedience, and positioning himself attentively to connect made it possible for the day's events to unfold in amazing, life-changing, and significant ways.

In many cases, the relational conditions or climate for a conversation, interaction, or divine opportunity might actually seem quite uninviting in the moment. All kinds of "small" issues can seem "significant" enough to deter obedience to a divine prompting—poor timing, external and internal distractions, disagreeable attitudes, and resistance by others. However, some people are still able to recognize divine promptings, still willing to obey God's desire for the moment, and they are still able to have a "small yet significant" impact on those around them.

These Christians, like the janitor, met and exceeded the small amount of connection that was possible for a difficult situation. After all, the janitor happened to be cleaning the woman's room during a rather intense and awkward relational climate. Many people in his position would have snuck quietly out the door and moved on to cleaning the next room. Perhaps they would have prayed for the woman as they went on with their work, but they wouldn't have taken the small but necessary steps to connect with David.

We must remember that, ultimately, the overall impact of our actions in these divine opportunities is up to God and God alone. All we can do is remain sensitive to our spiritual promptings, take relational risks (big or small), and allow God to do His will in His way. So please do not stress yourself out. Don't imagine you need to find a local TV station that will air your daily devotional program, and then scamper around the city hoping to run into someone who just prayed for God to send you to them.

Instead, ask God to show off His creativity and unique design with your individual circumstances. Let Him direct you and use you in big or small conversations with strangers, family members, friends, or colleagues. Listen for cues in conversation in everyday life that allude to possible needs and areas of attention. Do everything you can to break free from that growing trend to be apathetically-sympathetic. Follow up with people, listen intently, and ask them how you might be of assistance. And please do not forget about the small things you can do for the Lord by way of entertaining strangers in conversation—for by doing so you might just be entertaining angels (Hebrews 13:2). It was Mother Teresa who said, "Do small things with great love."

Bright Spots

Christians like David, the janitor, and all the others whose stories I'll share in chapters to come are examples of "bright spots" in relational engagement. Dan and Chip Heath, authors of *Switch: How to Change Things When Change is Hard*, refer to bright spots as "successful efforts worth emulating."[8] The bright spots that I have analyzed in my research include a wide range of divine opportunity success stories. Despite the variations between people, time, places, topics, and issues, I was still able to discover patterns and consistencies of divine opportunities and personal efforts worth emulating.

The "bright spot approach" to divine opportunities has resulted in several discoveries, most of which are scattered throughout the following chapters. The first discovery that I would like to share involves a comparison between Christians who are skilled in recognizing and acting upon *divine* opportunities and "lucky people" who are skilled at recognizing and acting upon *chance* opportunities.

Dr. Richard Wiseman, author of *The Luck Factor*, conducted a ten-year study of "lucky" and "unlucky" people in order to distinguish the differences between them. As a result, Dr. Wiseman identified four principles that were consistent among people who considered themselves "lucky." His research shows that there is no such thing as being lucky or unlucky; rather, people's experiences are dependent upon how they see the world, their ability or inability to recognize opportunities, and their courageous or timid responses to such opportunities. Based upon my research of divine opportunities and observations of "bright spot Christians," these same principles hold true for Christians who consistently recognize and capitalize on divine opportunities.

The distinguishing difference between Dr. Wiseman's work and my own is that Dr. Wiseman suggests that "good fortune is less about supernatural forces, and more about a positive attitude."[9] I, on the other hand, suggest that divine opportunities are very much dependent upon both God's divine influence and our positive attitude and faithful obedience to that influence.

Dr. Wiseman's four principles of "lucky" people will be presented below and adapted to illustrate these ideas. The people to whom Dr. Wiseman refers to as "lucky," I refer to as observant, optimistic, obedient Christians, or abbreviated as Triple O Christians.

Principle One

"Lucky people create, notice and act upon the chance opportunities in their lives."[10]

Triple O Christians create, notice, and act upon the divine opportunities in their lives.

Triple O Christians take risks socially, engaging with the world, and they expect God to do His will. These Christians are open to new experiences and they accept the relational invitations of others as a gift of opportunity, whether it's for coffee and conversation or for serving the homeless downtown. Regardless of the experience or the situation in which they find themselves, Triple O Christians remain attentive to the divine promptings of God.

Principle Two

"Lucky people make successful decisions by using their intuition and gut feelings."[11]

Triple O Christians make successful decisions by using their divine intuition and spiritual feelings.

Regardless of the experience, new and unique or mundane and routine, Triple O Christians are mindful of, and obedient to, divine promptings and spiritual hunches. Furthermore, these Christians seek to enhance their spiritual intuition by spending intimate time connecting with God. Most of these

Christians do so by reading the Bible or praying, and, more specifically, praying for divine opportunities. Pastor Chris Lewis recently reiterated a great suggestion: "If you want to hear God speak to you, read your Bible. If you want to hear God speak to you in an audible voice, read it out loud."

Principle Three

"Lucky people's expectations about the future help them fulfill their dreams and ambitions."[12]

Triple O Christians' expectations about the future help them fulfill their divine opportunities.

Triple O Christians expect God to bless them with divine opportunities. Even in the presence of unlikely situations and circumstances, Triple O Christians can anticipate the possibility of a divine opportunity. These Christians are not trying to force divine opportunities, but they're open to God's prompting in whatever situation they find themselves. They are willing to test the relational waters whenever they sense an opportunity might be upon them. Furthermore, Triple O Christians are optimistic that God can bless any interaction, and they don't underestimate the potential of any given moment.

Principle Four

"Lucky people are able to transform their bad luck into good fortune."[13]

With God's help, Triple O Christians are able to transform bad situations into divine opportunities.

Triple O Christians are confident that what the devil meant for harm, God can use for good. Joseph said to his brothers after undergoing years of painful circumstances: "You intended to harm me, but God intended it for good to accomplish what is now being done, the saving of many lives"

(Genesis 50:20). These Christians are capable of turning a bad situation into a positive experience. Their attitude and approach provide them with opportunities to save a conversation or alter the endings of what would normally be negative, or neutral, experiences.

Additionally, Triple O Christians have a tendency to recognize and learn from their past missed opportunities in order to increase the likelihood that they will seize similar opportunities in the future. We are commanded by God to be strong and courageous in the midst of missed opportunities: "Have I not commanded you? Be strong and courageous. Do not be terrified; do not be discouraged, for the Lord your God will be with you wherever you go" (Joshua 1:9). Here are some questions to consider:

- How badly do you want the life of a Triple O (observant, optimistic, obedient) Christian?
- What have you done up to this point to achieve that life for yourself?
- What will it take for you to think, believe, and act consistently like a Triple O Christian?

Need an extra dose of motivation? In addition to the four modified principles above, Triple O Christians all have one thing in common: they have a full "manna jar."

What is a Manna Jar?

Moses said, "This is what the Lord has commanded: 'Take an omer of manna and keep it for the generations to come, so they can see the bread I gave you to eat in the desert when I brought you out of Egypt.'"

So Moses said to Aaron, "Take a jar and put an omer of manna in it. Then place it before the Lord to be kept for the generations to come." (Exodus 16:32–33)

The same way the Israelites were provided with manna to eat as they wandered through the desert, God will provide you with divine opportunities and answered prayers. Our individual "manna jars" are a place for us to store symbols and remembrances of our divine appointments and answered prayers. The Triple O (observant, optimistic, obedient) Christians of this world have an overflowing manna jar that is filled with tangible reminders of divine promptings, risk taking, optimistic obedience, faith-building experiences, and answered prayers.

David first brought this idea of the manna jar to my attention a few years ago. Occasionally, when David goes to preach, he will take his own manna jar up with him, and during the sermon he will take out an object, show it to the congregation, and then share the divine opportunity or answered prayer that the object represents.

You can do the same thing in your own life too. Create a manna jar for you and your family. Each time you or a family member experiences a divine opportunity or answered prayer, find a small object that represents that experience or godly provision and store it in your manna jar. These physical tokens can prompt you and your family members to reflect upon the many ways that God has provided for you over the years. Furthermore, you can use them as object lessons to help you "show and tell" stories of God's grace. Keep the manna jar in your home or office, and when people come to visit, they will see it and inevitably ask about it. That is your cue to take an object out and share the divine opportunity with them.

I keep a manna jar in my office. I have it placed right on the corner of my desk, and most people who find their way into my office will inevitably ask, "What's a manna jar?" Think about it. If you were in someone's home or office and they had a large container labeled "Manna Jar" in big letters on the front, wouldn't you ask the same question? The beauty of the manna jar is that it is a noninvasive way to share your God moments with both Christians and non-Christians alike. After all, they are the ones who asked about it. As David once told me, "People can debate theology with you, but they can't debate your personal experiences."

Do you want the life of an observant, optimistic, obedient Triple O Christian, and a full manna jar to go with it? In the chapters to come, the divine opportunities of our "bright spot Christians" will be broken down and analyzed for the purpose of offering you some specific recommendations and challenges to move you toward filling your manna jar. Your fears, worries, and concerns about taking relational risks with others will be put into manageable challenges for change.

Your job now is to find two accountability partners who are willing to read this book along with you and who will commit to adapting the Chapter Challenges into your daily or weekly routines. These accountability partners are vital to keep you committed to reading and working through the coming challenges. If you can get a life group, growth group, or discipleship group (or whatever you crazy kids are calling them nowadays) to join in this reading, that would be even better.

The writer of Ecclesiastes reminds us: "Two are better than one, because they have a good return for their work: If one falls down, his friend can help him up. But pity the man who falls and has no one to help him up." (Ecclesiastes 4:9–10)

Tasks and
Discussion Questions

1. Create your own manna jar for your home or office. Have some fun with it. Perhaps even make it eye-catching enough so that it will attract the attention of guests in your home or office so that they will be tempted to ask you about it.

2. Think of one noteworthy divine moment you have been a part of in the past that you could put in your manna jar. Either write the story down on a sheet of paper or find an object that will remind you of that particular experience and put it in the manna jar.

3. Which of the four principles do you have the easiest time living out? Which of the four principles do you struggle with the most? What steps could you take to live out these Triple O principles in your life?

Part One
Recognizing Divine Promptings

Be wise in the way you act toward outsiders; make the most of every opportunity. Let your conversation be always full of grace, seasoned with salt, so that you may know how to answer everyone.

—Colossians 4:5–6

Cultivating your ability to recognize divine promptings may be one of the most important spiritual skills you could ever develop. Recognizing divine promptings in the midst of busy daily life will help you avoid missing divine opportunities and will allow you to act with greater emotional and spiritual intelligence in life's various moments.

In the following chapters, there will be further elaboration upon two common types of promptings: spiritual promptings and situational promptings. Both of these promptings are recurring in the stories of divine opportunities. The promptings act like divine clues that God drops into people's lives in an attempt to lead them to obvious and not-so-obvious conversational opportunities. It takes a particular type of approach to living intentionally and allowing for spontaneity so that people can develop a sixth sense for seeing the unseen and hearing the unheard, as to respond to subtle promptings toward relational moments.

This may seem a bit odd, but I want you to take ten seconds to look at the following picture and count the number of squares that you see. You can either approximate the ten seconds or you can set a timer on your phone to keep you honest.

So how many squares did you see? Did you see between twenty and fifty squares? Now let me ask you this, without looking back at the picture, how many circles did you see? Were you too focused on counting the squares that you overlooked the circles?

Let's think of it this way. All the squares represent daily items on our to-do list and schedule—all of our personal tasks, errands, work responsibilities, meetings, places to be, and things to do. After all, these items are the ones that highjack our attention for the majority of each day. The circles, on the other hand, represent the divine opportunities that God may be presenting us with each day. The problem is that we get so focused on the square tasks that we completely overlook all of the circle divine opportunities, even though the circles are right there scattered amidst those squares you counted so quickly. When we are busy moving from task to task or meeting to meeting, we can completely lose sight of the opportunities for possible connection and outreach as we transition from point A to point B or task A to task B.[14]

Most of you are busy people, so of course you can't afford to just wander through your day waiting and looking for the next divine opportunity as you skip meetings or school to do so. If you did meander through life and ignore all your commitments, you would eventually get fired from your job or fail your classes. The key is to live intentionally and allow for spontaneity. You can live intentionally by waking up with a game plan, a schedule in place, and a to-do list on hand. However, you must also be willing to allow for spontaneity. You must be flexible and open to God occasionally disrupting that daily agenda to care for those you come across in your daily walk, even if it is just for an extra sixty seconds of undivided, attentive, active listening in conversation that lets someone feel truly listened to and acknowledged.

Part of this act of recognizing divine opportunities might require you to reconsider what you would count as a divine opportunity. In a recent survey conducted with the assistance of my communication students, we asked 204 participants, "How many divine opportunity conversations have you experienced in the past year?" The answer options included: (a) None, (b) between 1–10, (c) between 10–20, or (d) 20 or more. The results were interesting. There were two large groups of responses. The largest group of 58 percent (119 out of 204) identified between one to ten divine opportunities in the past year, while the second largest group of 21 percent (43 out of 204) identified twenty or more divine opportunities in the past year.

The rationale behind these two significant sets of responses could be explained by the fact that people have varying views of what constitutes a divine opportunity. There seem to be two camps, one group of people who view divine opportunities as both *small and large acts* of moments of connection, which might explain the 21 percent who identified twenty or more divine opportunities in the last year. There's also a second group of people who view divine opportunities as *only large acts* of connection, which might explain the largest group of 58 percent that identified between one to ten divine opportunities in the last year.

In light of these findings, the first step in recognizing divine promptings and opportunities may be to acknowledge that divine opportunities come in all conversational shapes and sizes. As discussed in the previous chapter, don't forget about the small things you can do for others, for what may seem like a small moment to you may be a pivotal moment to someone else. What may seem like a small amount of extra attention paid to someone in conversation may be the only act of true acknowledgment they receive that day.

Chapter 3
Prompted by the Spirit

If we live by the Spirit, let us also walk by the Spirit.

—Galatians 5:25 NASB

For those who live according to the flesh set their minds on the things of the flesh, but those who live according to the Spirit set their minds on the things of the Spirit. For to set the mind on the flesh is death, but to set the mind on the Spirit is life and peace. For the mind that is set on the flesh is hostile to God, for it does not submit to God's law; indeed, it cannot. Those who are in the flesh cannot please God. You, however, are not in the flesh but in the Spirit, if in fact the Spirit of God dwells in you.

—Romans 8:5–9 ESV

A Divine Opportunity

Larry, a sixty-five-year-old retiree, shared the following divine opportunity that occurred about thirty years prior to the time of the interview. This particular divine opportunity was so powerful that it still stands out in his mind as a wonderful testimony of how God uses him to minister to others. This is a great example of how God leads us and guides us through spiritual promptings. He writes:

> In 1983, I was living and working in Memphis, Tennessee. This particular day, I was driving home from work along highway 240 on the south side of Memphis. Along the drive, I saw a car pulled over on the side of the highway, pointed in the direction of my travel, with someone standing off to the side of the car. The moment I saw this person I had this impulse to pull over and help. Before I could even weigh my options, I had another strong feeling that I needed to pull over. In that moment, when I spotted the car off the side of the highway, I felt like I was sensing God's voice and instruction. It wasn't a voice out of heaven or even an audible voice for that matter—it wasn't anything like that. In fact, I've never really had that. It was more of an internal presence of God. It was as if I was hearing God's voice in my spirit; it's like I had to get over, I had to pull off and help. I've driven by stranded cars before, but I didn't feel this way. I hadn't even had time to identify that it was a woman or anything else about the situation itself that would have compelled me. It was outside myself and it was outside the situation, that this compelling force caused me to know that I needed to stop.
>
> I pulled over on the shoulder about a hundred yards behind the car and coasted up behind it. And there I found this young female, in her mid-twenties, standing beside her car, which had a flat tire on the right rear side. She was just standing there gazing off into the distance, like she was checked out. I approached her and asked her if she needed help. She just turned and looked at me with a dazed look on her face. And then out of nowhere she just rushed into my arms and broke down crying, sobbing crying, and opening up about her life circumstances and all that was going on.
>
> She told me that she had just come from St. Jude's Hospital where her two-year-old son was being treated for leukemia, and that she was staying with her parents because her husband had recently walked out on her and their ill child. In this moment, it was like she was just so overwhelmed by life and so flooded with emotion that she just couldn't keep it together any longer. It didn't seem to matter at all that I was a complete stranger. She was just so vulnerable and so distraught about her young two-

year-old son having to battle leukemia and what she was to do now as a single parent.

However, even though I was a stranger, it all began to make perfect sense. You see, I had lost my first wife about eight and a half years earlier to leukemia right there in Memphis, and at the time of this opportunity I also had a two-year-old son with my second wife. So this was an opportunity God had orchestrated for me to open up and share with her about my experience and share with her a level of understanding and empathy that no one else along that stretch of highway could have. It was a God thing. I don't recall a lot of what I said—it's like it came in and went out, a lot like a gift of the Spirit. It's not necessarily something I thought about and said. It just flowed. I felt an anointing or empowerment as I was talking with her. And I felt like she was receiving what she needed through what I said. Her breaking down and crying was perhaps a release from the kind of the detached frustration, almost like she didn't know what to do or had even given up.

After holding her, talking with her, and changing her tire, I asked if I could pray for her. Before I prayed, however, I asked her for the name of her son, and as soon as I asked I immediately knew what she was going to say. Sure enough, she said that her son's name was Aaron, which was the same name as my two-year-old son. The overlap of our stories was amazing, with our sons having the same name and being the same age, and with her son being in a similar health situation as my first wife, with leukemia. I never asked for her name, I just held her while she cried. And then I prayed with her. I wished her God's help and God's speed, and she drove off down the road.

When I got back in my car and started down the road, I was weeping and emotional. It took me back to the things that had happened in my life and some of the ways that God helped me and ministered to me during my wife's time with leukemia. I felt His presence at different times during my wife's illness, so there was a tumbling of memories that it brought about. But, ultimately, this built confidence in my ability to recognize the voice of God. I drove away with a greater awareness and obedience to the gentle nudges from God. And instead of just blowing it off or thinking, "Oh, that's just me," I became more trusting of hearing God and being submissive to what He wants me to do.

What a remarkable story of a divine opportunity where God orchestrated the meeting of two strangers for one goal—the comfort and support of a frightened and distraught mother in a desperate time of need. If it weren't for Larry's quick spiritual instinct and reaction, this moment and compassionate exchange could have resulted in something far less remarkable and far less comforting for this young mother. Should Larry have second-guessed his gut instinct, this woman could have ended up with a less than empathetic roadside assist. She could have been greeted by someone who would have been startled and unresponsive to her emotional breakdown, they could have been put off by the over-sharing of personal details, and they could have fixed her tire but left her emotionally deflated.

We have all found ourselves in situations where we experienced this sixth sense—gut instincts, internal feelings, or spiritual promptings. These promptings can lead to one of four scenarios. One, we respond to these promptings and experience something unique and faith building. Two, we respond to these promptings and are left feeling unfulfilled or led astray. Three, we ignore these promptings and are none the wiser to what may or may not have been. Or four, we ignore these promptings and later realize the consequences of the missed opportunity.

Unfortunately, too many people have had to learn the hard lesson that results from scenario number four of ignoring a prompting only to later realize the negative afterlife of that missed opportunity. This chapter addresses this issue of how to recognize and entertain our spiritual promptings, and how to enter into a lifestyle of this sixth-sense living.

Our Sixth Sense: The Spiritual X Factor

Intuition experts, such as Alden Hayashi, have referred to the gut instinct as the X factor of emotional intelligence.[15] Hayashi described this X factor as "an uncanny ability to detect patterns, perhaps subconsciously, that other people either overlook or mistake for random noise."[16] The first step is to detect and recognize signposts and cues that often fall outside of one's consciousness. The second step, called cross-indexing, takes this gut instinct to the next level. Cross-indexing occurs when we recognize how the subconscious signal or clue connects to a seemingly unrelated moment or experience. Ultimately, those who excel in utilizing the X factor are those who are able to recognize and connect the subconscious dots in everyday life.

As Christians we might come to understand this X factor, gut instinct, as the Spirit of God that resides and lives inside each of us. Romans 8:9 states that "the Spirit of God dwells in you." Perhaps the response of our gut in-stinct is actually the awakening or arousing of the Holy Spirit living inside us. And God is calling us out of the mundane nature and course of our daily living through spiritual promptings, nudgings, and stirrings inside our hearts, guts, and minds that ignite the spiritual X factor.

Linking this to the Triple O Christians, who are observant, optimistic, and obedient, these are Christians who have that uncanny ability to de-tect patterns that other people overlook or mistake for random noise. The Triple O Christians are then able to connect those often overlooked cues to their current experiences, and, thus, engage in a fleeting moment that might have otherwise been missed. In order to follow in the footsteps of Triple O Christians, we need to open ourselves up to the many ways that God triggers our own spiritual X factor.

Spiritual Bids

How does God awaken our spiritual X factor? One of the ways is through *spiritual bids*. I have adapted the term "spiritual bids" from what relation-ship expert Dr. John Gottman calls *emotional bids*.[17] Gottman has spent forty years researching and writing about romantic relationships, and one of the fundamental principles of his work includes the core element for closeness and how partners reach out to one another through emotional bids for attention. Gottman states, "That basic idea has to do with the way people, in mundane moments in everyday life, make attempts at emotional communication, and how others around them respond, or fail to respond, to these attempts."[18]

In terms of personal relationships, these bids could include (1) an invita-tion to lunch, (2) inquiring about one's day in hopes that the other person would reciprocate the question and allow them to open up about their day, or (3) simply a deep sigh in hopes that someone asks if he or she is okay. In the same way, God regularly makes spiritual bids for our attention through internal promptings, which we either recognize or miss. And if recognized, we either respond to or ignore these bids for attention. God's spiritual bids may also include a wide range of obvious or subtle requests for attention, such as (1) a gut feeling, (2) a fleeting thought about a loved one or friend, or (3) a recalling of Scripture.

Recognizing Spiritual Bids

Once we acknowledge that God makes such spiritual bids, the next step is recognizing those bids in the context of everyday life. One strategy for learning how to recognize God's spiritual bids is to analyze how God has made spiritual bids to you in the past. What do these spiritual bids look like, feel like, or sound like to you personally? Is it a feeling in your gut, a reoccurring thought in your mind, or a pounding in your chest? Do you tend to recognize spiritual bids while reading the Bible, through the words and actions of your conversational partners, or in the midst of prayer? The primary goal for developing this radar for spiritual promptings is to recognize the many ways God has reached out to you in the past so that you can recognize similar spiritual bids in the future. Yet it is also important to be careful not to limit God to only those promptings that are familiar, but also to be open to new and unique ways that God may call you out and into relationship with others.

One practical strategy you may want to try comes from Gottman's work with recognizing and responding to emotional bids through an exercise titled Become Collectors of Emotional Moments.[19] Gottman states, "Many people start the day with certain goals in mind—to exercise, to eat a healthy diet, to meet a performance standard at work, and so on. Try adding this one to your list: 'Collect at least three emotional moments.' Then, at the end of your day, look back and see how you did."[20]

I would like to suggest that we become collectors of spiritual moments, that we wake up ready and alert in an attempt to collect at least three spiritual moments throughout our day, and at the end of the day we reflect upon how we did, with whom we connected, or in what moments we recognized God's presence. These moments don't all have to come in the form of conversation with others, and they may not even be divine opportunities in the same sense as they have been discussed up to this point. In fact, a spiritual moment may just be a feeling of connection through a sunset, a loving embrace with your child, or experiencing laughter with friends. The main purpose of this activity is to simply open your eyes and ears to the divine possibilities in everyday life, to recognize God's presence in and around you, and to learn to discern, trust, and be obedient to such spiritual bids for your attention.

God's Bidding

There is a striking difference between relational partners' emotional bids and God's spiritual bids. When we ignore or reject the emotional bids of other people, the probability that the other person will attempt to rebid once ignored or rejected is unlikely. In fact, as we continue to ignore or reject the emotional bids of others, the bidding will eventually cease. Whereas, with God, even if we ignore or reject His spiritual bids, He will continue to pursue us our entire lives. We can choose to ignore God's bids, but there isn't anything we can do to keep Him from pursuing us.

The following story is about a man named Jim, a sixty-one-year-old president of a leadership institute. Jim's story is an incredible testimony of how God continues to reach out to us with spiritual bids and spiritual promptings even though we have chosen to ignore similar bids in the past.

> Years back, I was volunteering at a weekend-long church retreat called a Cursillo. While at the retreat I was working with a group of volunteers who were in charge of the dining setup, food preparation, and service for the weekend. In this group, there was a woman named Barbra who had suffered a stroke and as a result she had lost the use of a vast majority of her right side. This caused her many physical complications, in addition to her speech being severely impaired. Over the course of a couple days, the group of us volunteers had grown to know one another quite well, and I had developed a friendship with Barbra. On Saturday night, the second of the three-day retreat, we were gathering around and just kind of resting in a hallway. We were all talking to Barbra and she was saying that she wasn't making any progress and the stroke was really hard for her. It was causing her to feel sad and depressed.
>
> In that moment, talking about her stroke, I felt God instructing me to lay my hands on her and pray for her healing. That thought about praying for healing Barbra never crossed my mind until that time. We had been sitting there for half an hour or so when that thought hit me. I thought I would be embarrassed, I thought she would think I was crazy and that everybody else would think I was crazy too. I thought that laying hands on people was weird, and I didn't pray for her healing because I didn't believe I could.
>
> The next day, the thought was still on my mind, even though I'd kind of put it off because I thought it was just a passing, silly thought. That was until Sunday afternoon when I met up with my friend, who was my coleader, and she said to me, "Jim, I gotta ask you something. Last night, when we were talking to Barbra, I felt like we could have laid our hands on her and God would have healed her." I just looked at Debbie and I started to cry. I said, "My God, Debbie, I felt the same thing." We just sort of stood there and looked at each other, crying. It was awful. It just hit me, like she shot me right in the heart. The more we

started talking, the more I realized God could have healed her. But we also realized that the moment passed and we had missed our chance. Debbie felt as badly as I did.

The following week I had a meeting with my spiritual mentor. By this time, I had already gotten over it a bit. I said to my mentor, "Wasn't that stupid to think that God would have used me to heal her? You know, God has never given me the gift of healing before and I don't know what prompted me to think that He would this time." My spiritual mentor, who was a pretty tough cookie, said to me, "What did you have to lose? Would you have been embarrassed? Were you going to make her worse? You know, Jim, when God moves, you move." I just started crying because I felt so bad. Then she said, "Well, maybe you should feel bad." And I did. For me, it was like a little boy being punished. Only my punishment was the guilt. He laid that on my heart—how could I have not done this? So ever since then, I don't question that—when the Spirit says to act, I act.

My mentor never let me off the hook. She said, "You know, you can't be afraid. What's the possible damage?" I mean it's not like I'm telling somebody to jump off a cliff or anything. Certainly, I wasn't ever going to make her any worse. My wife believes in the power of laying on hands and praying for people. I didn't believe that too much. In fact, I didn't believe it at all. That's why it was so strange for me for God to prompt me in this way. And, you know, now, sure! Sure I will, because I have learned that you never know what God's going to do. Just do what He says; He'll do the rest. If He wants you to lay hands on people and pray, then do it. If nothing happens, well, that's up to God. That's not up to you.

It clearly impacted me that when I feel like God is telling me to act, I do. I don't dismiss people who believe in the laying on of hands and healing. I believe that some have it and some don't. Who am I to limit God?

Two years later though, I was at Cursillo again, but this time I was giving a talk. For my talk I decided to tell people about my experience with Barbra. My main message that day was this: "If you have a chance to act on behalf of Jesus, then take it." I told the room about Barbra through my tears. Choking it back, I said, "If I ever had the chance to tell Barbra how sorry I was, and how I wish she could be healed so much, I would." Although, it never dawned on me to go see her. I just couldn't. I felt too embarrassed.

Well, about two years after the talk, which was about four years after the prompting to pray for Barbra's healing, I found myself on a new committee at our church. There were six of us on this committee in all. Upon arriving early at the first meeting, one of my friends who was on the committee said, "Jim, here's the list of people coming today." And there was Barbra's name. She was on the committee too. I just closed my eyes, and I was so scared. You know, when it feels like you've hurt somebody, and now you're going to see them for the first time and you didn't have the guts to apologize. I remember saying, "Lord, I have to apologize to this woman."

One of the people said, "You know Barbra, don't you?" I reluctantly said, "Yes, I do." Then she said, "When I told Barbra you were on the committee, she was so happy to see you. She had gotten a tape of your talk from the Cursillo," which, of course, I didn't know. She continued, "She got a tape of your talk, and she said it changed her life."

This was so unbelievable! This still gets me even to this day.

Just then Barbra walked in, greeted me, and told me that was one of the nicest things anybody had ever done for her—ever. She wanted me to know that she listened to the tape of my talk over and over again. Barbra said, "I began to get stronger and stronger. My speech began to come back. And now, here I am."

Shortly after she got the tape, she got dramatically better! She regained the use of her right side and her speech improved. She was healed! At this time, you would've known that she had some sort of incident, but she had the use of her right side and her foot wasn't dragging anymore, and her speech was much better. She could clearly speak. She would never fully recover, but she was dramatically better!

Every chance that I get, for the last fourteen or fifteen years of my life, when I've had a chance to do something, by God— literally by God—I'll do it. I just felt so incredibly bad after that incident. Then I felt so incredibly good. It was like, "Oh, thank you! Thank you, thank you!"

That was one of the most convicting times of my life, with Barbra. It was also one of the biggest redemptions I have ever had in my life. So that was my divine opportunity, that God gave me a second chance. One, He convicted me, and then four years later He redeemed me. But before the redemption could take place, He clearly let me understand what a mistake I had made. Then He had me publicly admit it, and after I was able to confess my cowardice, or my lack of cooperation more than anything, He used that to heal her.

And I also, in a big way, learned about redemption through the whole incident. He taught me a hard lesson, and by His mercy He redeemed me from that, which I love to tell people. I say, "Listen. I was in the pits. And He showed me the lesson; here's what happens when you don't do what God tells you, and here is how He loves you enough to redeem you from that."

A God of Rebidding

I love the fact that we serve a God who will continue to rebid time and time again. We serve a God who will rebid no matter how many times we choose to ignore or reject His bids. Thankfully, we serve a God who is bigger, better, and more persistent than our human counterparts, who, if ignored or rejected as many times as we do with God, would cut us off and cease to continue to seek us. Jim's story is such a testament to the fact that even when we ignore God's initial bids for our attention, He continues to stick with us and send bids for life-giving course correction.

My favorite part about Jim's story is that he ultimately ends up transforming into a Triple O Christian. However, he wouldn't have ever reached that place if it weren't for the original missed opportunity, a recognition of that missed opportunity, and course-correcting punishment of guilt and conviction. Without Jim's painful yet teachable missed opportunity, he would have never been motivated to this level of action. Without the transformative experience that resulted from rejecting God's initial spiritual bidding, Jim would have likely been a Christian who only responded to bids when they were within reason. But, because of his painful experience, he was able to get to a place of responding to God's bids even when those bids call him out of his comfort zone.

Discussion Questions

1. In what ways have you experienced spiritual promptings in the past?
2. What are some ways you could take time throughout your day to open yourself up to God's spiritual bidding?
3. If you were in Jim's shoes, how would you have responded to his initial missed opportunity?

Spiritual Bidding Task

Each day this week:
1. Collect at least three spiritual moments.
2. Reflect upon these spiritual moments at the end of the day.
3. Share at least one of these spiritual moments with a friend, family member, roommate, or coworker. And ask them if they have experienced any spiritual promptings or moments themselves.

Chapter 4

Prompted by the Situation

Now Moses was tending the flock of Jethro his father-in-law, the priest of Midian, and he led the flock to the far side of the desert and came to Horeb, the mountain of God. There the angel of the Lord appeared to him in flames of fire from within a bush. Moses saw that though the bush was on fire it did not burn up. So Moses thought, "I will go over and see this strange sight—why the bush does not burn up."

—Exodus 3:1–3

A Divine Opportunity

Vaughn, a forty-two-year-old construction services salesman, shared a divine opportunity he experienced about fifteen years earlier. This divine interaction was a result of noticing and commenting on a T-shirt a customer was wearing while out on a sales call. This is an incredible testimony of someone who picked up on a situational prompting, in this case a logo on a T-shirt, and how it led to a divine opportunity.

In 1997, I was traveling through the Midwest on various sales calls. At this time, I was working as a salesperson for a cabinet design computer software company. We sold computers and software that allowed companies to design and demonstrate, in 3D, what customers' cabinets would look like in their homes.

On this particular day, I was driving to a town near Cincinnati to meet a potential client. I was in a rush to catch the guy before he left for the evening. I arrived shortly after 6:00 pm, and as I walked up to the door it appeared as if I had missed everyone and the shop had closed. However, after some intense knocking on the front door, I finally saw this guy in the back who heard my knocking and turned and started to walk toward the door. As he was initially turned away from me, I could see that he was wearing a T-shirt with the logo for the Royal Rangers on the back. If you don't know, the Royal Rangers are essentially the Boy Scouts for the Assemblies of God denomination.

As he answered the door, I introduced myself and I asked him if he was a Royal Ranger. Todd said that he was actually a part-time youth pastor and Royal Ranger leader. I told him that I was a Royal Ranger from way back and also a part of the Assemblies of God denomination.

At this time in my life, I had just recently returned from a church revival I had attended, which completely changed my life and transformed my faith. When we got on the topic of Royal Rangers and our shared denomination, I couldn't help but tell him a little bit about the revival and my experience attending it. However, I also had a job to do and a sale to make, so I didn't get too far into the story.

Todd invited me in and we got settled so that I could go through my usual sales pitch, which, by the way, was typically a rather difficult sale because the computers and software were expensive; we're talking several thousand dollars each. But to my surprise, he stopped me after just five minutes of my pitch and said, "Great! I'll take two computers and two sets of programming, one for this store and one for our store a few towns away. Now tell me more about this revival." This really took me back, in a good way of course. I had never had a sale this quick or this easy before.

Right then and there our conversation shifted from cabinets and computers back to the revival and my experience. I shared with him what I encountered, how it transformed my faith, and changed my outlook on life. Todd had question after question and he took such an interest in my whole experience. Before we knew it, it was midnight and I still had a three-hour drive back to my hotel. At this time, we scheduled an appointment for me to come back two weeks later to install the computers, the sftware, and to train two people, one person for each store.

Well, a couple of days before I was to return for the install and training, Todd called me up and asked me to bring some of the videos and materials that I had purchased while I was at the revival so that he could watch them and we could talk more about it all. As requested, I packed the materials and headed out. Right as I arrived at the store, Todd greeted me and told me that he was actually about to head into a meeting to quit his job there at the cabinet shop. He informed me that shortly after I left our first appointment, another church's pastor had retired and they asked him to take over as the pastor of their church. Although it was a small church of about forty people, they were going to be able to pay him a salary for the year. Todd had really been inspired and motivated by our first conversation and it moved him to take up this position in full-time ministry. And even though he was quitting that day, Todd said that he would still like to meet up and talk while I was in town for the install at their two stores.

We met up in the evenings after I finished each install and we would talk about our faith and what God was doing. And at the end of the two days, Todd told me he was going to make a trip to the revival and check it out for himself, which he ended up doing, and it affected him just as much as it did me.

About a year later, I was up in his area and I decided to stop by his church and see how he was doing. I dropped by his church, which was a small church in a strip mall location. When I arrived the receptionist greeted me and she informed me that Todd was across town at the time. She gave me directions to meet up with him and told me how excited Todd would be to see me and share with me all that had happened.

I immediately headed over in excitement to see and hear from Todd. Well, when I arrived, Todd was inside this old bowling alley working with some others on a construction project, and he rushed over to greet me and fill me in on what was happening. Todd, in a fit of enthusiasm, told me that when he went to the revival he had the same experience that I did. He said it was transformational—it transformed his faith—and he returned to his church with an overwhelming sense of the Holy Spirit. Todd said that when he returned, they started to experience a revival right there in their small-town church. His church had grown from about forty to four hundred, and some three hundred people had been saved at his church in the past year. With that increase in members and donations, they were able to buy the abandoned bowling alley and were renovating it into their new church building. It was the most incredible experience I have ever been blessed to be a part of.

I could hardly believe all that had happened for Todd and his church since our conversation a year earlier. Honestly, that conversation and experience carried me for months knowing that a simple conversation and interaction between cabinet guys changed an entire community. God used me! God used *me*—not a preacher, pastor, or an evangelist—but He used me, Vaughn, a simple software salesman to transform a pastor, who transformed a community. And the craziest part is that it all started with me seeing and responding to that emblem on the back of his shirt. Without me noticing that Royal Rangers emblem, I probably would have never brought up my faith or my experience at the revival. I simply would have gone into my sales pitch that night, made my sale, and driven right back out of town.

I love what Vaughn says about God using him, "a simple software sales-man." That line sums up the whole purpose of why I did this research and why I am writing this book. If you remember nothing else, don't forget that God uses *all* people regardless of their background, titles, jobs, degrees, or status. After all, "There are no gifted or ungifted here, only those who give themselves and those who withhold themselves."[21] And Vaughn most certainly recognized an opportunity for connection, which started with a Royal Rangers T-shirt, and he chose to give himself over to the moment.

Sensitivity to Situational Promptings

Just as God used a burning bush to get Moses's attention, He used a Royal Rangers T-shirt to get the attention of Vaughn that evening. As stated in Exodus 3:1–3, at the time of the burning bush experience, Moses was tending the flock of his father-in-law. In other words, Moses was out working tending to the sheep. Granted, I have never tended to a flock of my own before (other than my kids), but I would have to imagine that your attention would be spread thin and narrowly focused on the task at hand. Luckily for Moses, God was willing to get a little creative to get his attention and snap him out of his work routine of tending the flock. Moses's prompting by the burning bush is a great illustration and reminder that we cannot underestimate God's creativity in gaining our attention and directing our focus toward a divine task.

While we can all appreciate and admire God's supreme creativity, this does create a little bit of a challenge for us. For God may not always send us a sign as obvious as a burning bush along our path. Take Vaughn for example. His divine attention getter was much less obvious. Nonetheless, Vaughn spotted the Royal Rangers T-shirt and allowed it to highjack his attention and guide his conversation. What resulted from Vaughn's attention and response was truly inspiring. It would be a shame to think about the faith-building experience that Vaughn would have deprived himself of if he had not been cognizant enough to recognize the T-shirt, simply focused on his computer software sale, and withheld himself from the moment of connection between him and Todd.

Todd's Royal Rangers T-shirt is just one example of the many small, subtle situational promptings that God uses to try to direct our attention, focus, and, ultimately, our hearts. These situational cues could include any aspect of another person's attire, attitude, emotions, or mannerisms that gain our attention and prompt us toward conversation. For example, a subtle situational cue might include a tattoo on someone's arm that we notice and ask about only to discover a unique backstory that leads to deeper conversation than we would have anticipated. A cue could be a subtle emotional display of a momentary frown that we notice on our coworker's face across the cubical. Another could be a conflicting expression of verbal and nonverbal cues as our neighbor says she is doing fine, but her body language would lead us to believe otherwise. It could even be a stranger who reminds us of a friend and that resemblance prompts us to call that friend only to realize he or she is having a rough week and desperately needed someone to talk to.

These situational cues could also include any aspect of the environment that may grab our attention and pull us out of the ordinary routine of our day. A situational cue, in this sense, could be an unexpected twenty-minute break in the middle of our workday that leads to a conversation with a colleague when we go outside for fresh air. While another could come from taking a different route home from work one day, only to cross paths with an old friend. Actually, earlier today when I was editing this chapter in a coffee shop a gentleman commented on a "HE>i" sticker on the backside of my laptop and we ended up talking for an hour as I heard about and asked questions about this career, kids, divorce, budding stepfamily, and the like. It was a wonderful conversation that was a result of him stopping and making a comment about the sticker; without the sticker on my computer I doubt we would have ever said a word to each other.

The point is that we need to expand our understanding of how God may be reaching out to us in everyday life. I truly believe that God is regularly at work vying for our attention and that He is often going to great lengths to direct our focus toward others for reasons beyond our immediate understanding. And the bottom line is that we all have significant room for improvement in terms of expanding our social awareness of others, sensitivity to the emotional subtext of our conversations, and mindfulness of our environment. This next section, referencing a Good Samaritan Experiment, should be all the motivation you need to realize just how many divine opportunities we may be missing in everyday life.

The Good Samaritan Experiment

In Daniel Goleman's book *Social Intelligence*,[22] he summarizes an experimental research study that stands out in my mind as an incredibly powerful example of how even the most well-equipped and well-intentioned people are likely to overlook and neglect opportunities right in front of them. He writes:

> One afternoon at the Princeton Theological Seminary, 40 students waited to give a short practice sermon on which they would be rated. Half the students had been assigned random biblical topics. The other half had been assigned the parable of the Good Samaritan, who stopped to help a stranger by the roadside, an injured man ignored by people supposedly more "pious."
>
> The seminarians worked together in a room, and every 15 minutes one of them left to go to another building to deliver his sermon. None knew they were taking part in an experiment on altruism.
>
> Their route passed directly by a doorway in which a man was slumped, groaning in evident pain. Of the 40 students, 24 passed right by, ignoring the plaintive moans. And those who were mulling over the lessons of the Good Samaritan's tale were no more likely to stop and help than were any of the others.
>
> For the seminarians, time mattered. Among 10 who thought they were late to give their sermon, only one

stopped; among another 10 who thought they had plenty of time, six offered help.

Of the many factors that are at play in altruism, a critical one seems to be simply taking the time to pay attention; our empathy is strongest to the degree we fully focus on someone and so loop emotionally.

Simply paying attention allows us to build an emotional connection. Lacking attention, empathy hasn't a chance.[23]

Wow! That experimental study gets to me every time. Think about it for a moment: if these seminarians, who just spent the last half-hour preparing a sermon on the Good Samaritan, can manage to walk right past someone moaning in pain, then why would we be any different? And if you think you would be different, you're likely fooling yourself. As Goleman pointed out, the main factor at play was time.

We live in a society that is more pressed for time than at any point before in civilization. This experiment was first conducted back in 1973, so think about how much busier and more chaotic the average person's life has become since then. Most of us are constantly on the move from one thing to the next, so you can only imagine how many opportunities we have blown right by on our way to the next business meeting, sports practice, class, event, work shift, volunteer shift, music lesson, dance class, etc.

And if you didn't think the time factor was bad enough, just add in the cell phone factor as another distractor. In 1973, these seminarians weren't dilly-dallying around on their smart phones picking out an emoticon for their text message as they passed by the stranger moaning in pain. In actuality, they had fewer distractions at the time than we do now. Nowadays, as we race from one meeting to the next, one class to the next, one event to the next, we are typically filling any moment of downtime by engulfing ourselves in our cell phones. Even if we do have some downtime to shift our attention outward, we instead shift our attention downward into our phones, creating a terrible case of tunnel vision. It's not surprising to learn that by focusing on your phone for texting or reading you actually shrink your peripheral vision to one-tenth of its regular capacity in that moment.[24] This tunnel vision effect can account for quadrupling the number of walkers going to the hospital for injuries suffered from a person texting while walking. (Embarrassed to be a human yet? I am.)

Let me repeat the previous line from Goleman: "Simply paying attention allows us to build an emotional connection. Lacking attention, empathy hasn't a chance." Even the most kindhearted, compassionate, Bible reading, church attending, godly person hasn't a chance at connecting with someone emotionally if they never see them or notice them to begin with. While waking up every morning to read the Bible before you head out for the day is an incredible habit that should be cultivated, that act of godly focus is severely hampered if you head out for the day in a mode of go, go, go. More important than simply reading Scripture each morning is taking the time throughout your day to live out Scripture in relationship with others along your daily journey. Often we get so caught up in our day that we never stop and wait long enough to hear and see what or who God is placing before us.

Just think about who could be moaning in physical pain or sulking in emotional pain off in the other nine-tenths of our peripheral view that we are ignoring. As long as we are pressed for time or engulfed in our cell phones, then we are going to continue to miss a depressing number of situational cues God is dropping along our path each day.

Strategies for Increasing Your Social Awareness

I realize that for some of you, by talking bad about your cell phone it's like talking trash about your best friend. It's likely striking up some defensiveness, so I apologize. Actually, you know what, I don't apologize. There are far too many people who are all too consumed by their phones, and every now and again we need to keep those devices in our pocket and look around at the social world around us. We need to get outside the one-tenth of our cell phone field of view and start living and responding to what is occurring in the other nine-tenths of our periphery. There very well could be someone off in the other nine-tenths that would love for us to make them the focal point of our tunnel vision. Let's reserve our tunnel vision for people, not cell phones.

In their book *Emotional Intelligence 2.0*,[25] Bradberry and Greaves outline sixty-six strategies for increasing one's self-awareness, self-management, social awareness, and relationship management. I would like to share a few of those that I think could greatly improve our social awareness and our ability to notice and respond to situational promptings from God.

Take a Fifteen-Minute Tour

When you find yourself with a fifteen-minute break in your day, go on a walk around your office, campus, school, neighborhood, park, or wherever you happen to find yourself at that moment. We have quickly grown accustomed to filling any small break in our day, whether it's five minutes for fifteen minutes, with diving into our phones. We use that small break to check e-mail, catch up on news, scroll through social media feeds, or watch YouTube videos. Instead, I suggest that you pop your head up and open up your field of vision, take a walk, explore a new store, and challenge yourself to see and hear things you have never noticed before.

"Things to look for include the look and feel of people's workspaces, the timing of when different people move around the office, and which people seek interaction versus those who stay at their desks all day."[26] You may notice something about a colleague's workspace, like a picture you hadn't noticed before, that prompts a conversation between the two of you. You may notice someone roaming the office pretending to be doing something or looking for something when in reality they are just seeking conversation, a listening ear, or emotional support. Never underestimate how God could use you while out on a quick five to fifteen-minute tour.

Go People Watching

Who doesn't love to people watch? Humans are extraordinarily fascinating, entertaining, and engaging. After all, this is why we spend so much time on social media to begin with, because others provide us with all sorts of instant entertainment through their posts, pictures, and videos. However, what I am recommending is people watching in real-life rather than people watching through social media. Sit back and soak in your physical environment and those people who are around you who are live and in-person.

Use this time to hone your skills for reading others' emotions through their eyes, facial expressions, tone of voice, posture, gestures, timing, and intensity. This is a great opportunity to improve your ability to read people, and this will allow you to be more sensitive to similar responses and cues in conversation when needed. This could be a time when God brings someone to your attention through a subtle cue of a T-shirt, tattoo, smile, frown, tear, or laugh.

Catch the Mood of the Room

While you are out people watching and doing your quick assessment of nonverbal cues, including the eyes, facial expressions, tone of voice, posture, gestures, timing, and intensity, what you are essentially doing is catching the mood of the room or catching the mood of those you are watching. In doing so, you are improving your ability to read the emotional subtext of a conversation. After all, the words people use only make up about 7 percent of what they are fully communicating. The remaining 93 percent of what people are communicating is interpreted through their body language (55 percent) and their tone of voice (38 percent).

In order to properly interpret what someone says, then, we need to look far beyond their actual words; we need to look at the whole package of nonverbal cues, relationship cues, and contextual cues. You'd be surprised by how quickly and easily you can catch the mood of the room by simply "catching a whiff of an emotion in a smile or frown."[27] Once you have caught the mood of the room you may find that God provides you with a spiritual prompting to reach out to others through a thought in your mind, butterflies in your stomach, or a flutter in your heart.

Cell Phone Addiction Assessment

Below is an assessment for determining whether or not you may be addicted to your cell phone. According to the Diagnostic and Statistical Manual of Mental Disorders by the American Psychiatric Association,[28] addiction is prevalent when three or more of the following symptoms persist for at least twelve months. I challenge you to be brutally honest with yourself as you read through the following list of symptoms. Check the box for the following symptoms that have been consistent for the past twelve months. I have modified the language of the following substance abuse symptoms to fit the context of cell phone use. To clarify, cell phone use includes the use of e-mail, any social media viewing or activity, gaming, messaging, etc.:

- I often use my cell phone in larger stints or over longer periods of time than was intended when I pick it up.
- I have a persistent desire or unsuccessful efforts to cut down or control the use of my cell phone.
- I spend a great deal of time in activities (e.g., email, social media viewing, gaming, and/or messaging) for which my cell phone is necessary.
- I often have a strong urge to use my cell phone.

- The recurrent use of my cell phone often results in a failure to fulfill role obligations at work, school, or home.
- I continue to use my cell phone despite having persistent or recurrent social interpersonal problems caused or exacerbated by the effects of its use.
- Important social, occupational, or recreational activities are regularly given up or reduced because of the use of my cell phone.
- I have recurrent use of my cell phone even when it puts me in physical danger (e.g., texting while driving).
- I continue to use my cell phone despite knowledge of having a persistent or recurrent social or psychological problem that is likely to have been caused or exacerbated by my cell phone use.
- I have experienced an increased tolerance, resulting in growing need for more regular use of my cell phone.
- I regularly reach for my cell phone to relieve or avoid withdrawal symptoms.

How did you do and how do you rate?

> two to three symptoms = mild cell phone addiction
>
> four to five symptoms = moderate cell phone addiction
>
> six or more symptoms = severe cell phone addiction

Is it time for a cell phone detox period? I'm sure we could all use a little less time on our cell phones and more time with others face-to-face or at least voice-to-voice. Remember that thing called a phone call? Those were pretty cool. Phone calls aren't always as easy to navigate and maintain as texts, but sometimes they are exactly what's called for. We know this and yet we still avoid them. We have grown so accustomed to being able to craft a message on our own timetable using properly chosen words and phrases that we may fear the synchronicity of a phone conversation where we have to think on our feet and speak off the cuff. In the words of a weary and concerned journalist, "it's time for less tweeting, and more meeting."[29] How about you kick it old school this week and try to increase your phone calls and face-to-face conversations and decrease your text messages and posts.

Current research on technology use has noted that the average person checks their cell phone 150 times per day. That's crazy. What do you think your life would be like if you instead checked in with God 150 times per day?

I am willing to bet that not a single person will look back on their life and wish they had spent more time on their phone. In fact, as you look back on the last twelve months, do you wish you would have spent more or less time on your cell phone? How many people look back on the last year and think, "Oh man, I blew it. I wasted so much time in conversation with people that I could have spent tinkering around on my phone! What a wasted year."

Social and Situational Awareness

Now that you have some strategies to help open your eyes and ears to see the unseen and hear the unheard, I would like to share another divine opportunity story to help you better understand what these situational promptings might look like or feel like in everyday life. Unlike the spiritual promptings of the gut instincts and feelings, the situational promptings can vary drastically from person to person and situation to situation. Unlike Vaughn's T-shirt situational prompting, the following divine opportunity resulted from Darius, a twenty-one-year-old college student, bumping into a campus minster an unexplainable number of times over the course of his first two weeks of college.

> When I first got to college, as a freshman, my parents dropped me off on a Monday and I would say maybe two days later on a Wednesday the university had a midnight barbeque for all incoming freshman. This was a huge campus of about 30,000 students, so it was easy to get lost in the crowd, so the university set up this event to get people connected. I ended up walking down to the barbeque with a few other people I had met, and as I'm walking this guy off to the side of the road just kind of stopped me and said, "Hey, man, are you on the football team?" And I was like, "No, man, not at all." And really he just used that question to talk to me.
>
> Then he continued, "Yeah, you know my name is Lawrence and I'm a campus minister, and I just wanted to know if you are a Christian?" And I kind of blew him off. I was pretty cordial, but I just kind of blew him off, like, "Ehhh, I'm not really feeling that." But he gave me his number and I ended up throwing it away as soon as I got it because I was not going to call this guy. By the way, this guy was young—he didn't look like a campus pastor; he looked like a student. It turned out he had just graduated a year or two before.

Regardless, I figured that this was a big school; I was probably not going to run into this guy again. But as it turned out, I just kept running into him what seemed like every single day for two weeks. I bumped into him at a college fair where they sell posters. I saw him buying a poster, and we started talking again. The second time I bumped into him was when I was heading to get something to eat and I went past him and we stopped and chatted it up for a little bit. And then about the fourth or fifth time I thought, "Okay, I'm seeing this guy way too much."

One time I was coming out of class and he was walking down the sidewalk and before I walked out the door I stopped and stood there and watched him pass by. Then I walked the other way. I was sprinting almost, thinking I needed to get away from this guy. I would do that if I would see him—I would take the longest way possible to get to class. If he were on the path that would take me two minutes, I would take the five-minute route instead.

Then finally there was a time when he totally caught me off guard. It was like a sneak attack. I didn't see him coming at all. I was walking across a recreation field and I was talking to my friends and we were laughing and I heard somebody yell, "Darius." And I thought, "Oh crap." I just saw this guy way too much, he was everywhere on campus—he either had a twin or he was literally stalking me. I was not comfortable with that; I didn't know how I felt with another man stalking me. Finally, he said, "How is it that out of all the thousands of people on this campus you and I keep bumping into each other? There's got to be a reason we keep bumping into each other; let's get together for a Bible study."

He ended up inviting me to these Bible talks that I eventually went to. Then we ended up having personal Bible studies. And I also ended up going to his church. I just felt like God sort of set it up. Over the course of the last couple of years, Lawrence showed me a whole new side to Christianity. He taught me what it meant that Christ died for my sins, and he helped me realize that God wants to have a personal, intimate relationship with me. Because, growing up, my pop made me go to church and my parents forced me into faith, but I just ignored it and figured it was just something for old, boring people. But Lawrence showed me a whole new side to the faith. And for the first time, I really started to engage with it.

It was just crazy, because now the guy is one of my best friends. I was actually the usher in his wedding. And eventually I ended up getting baptized for real, on March 2, 2008. I will never forget that day—it was just a good day—I felt like for the first time this was my faith, this was my decision, and this was going to be my own personal relationship with God. It wasn't forced on me, and I didn't feel like it was governed by my parents. It was pretty cool, it was probably the best…yeah, it was definitely *the* best decision that I've made. But I think I would have missed it if I hadn't kept bumping into him and he hadn't kept asking me and inviting me to join him.

God's Pursuit and the Good Samaritan

Darius is such a fun young man, a total character, and entertaining to be around. God definitely sent a particular young man after him who could break through Darius's guard and defensiveness. Darius's divine opportunity highlights much of what has been discussed in this chapter. In particular, we notice Lawrence, the Good Samaritan, reaching out to Darius. Obviously, Darius wasn't lying on the side of the road writhing in physical pain, but it's almost as if Lawrence noticed the spiritual and emotional pain that Darius didn't even notice yet himself. But Lawrence was sensitive to God's pursuit of Darius. Both Darius and Lawrence recognized that they were crossing paths an unusual amount, which was their situational prompting. Lawrence acted on that prompting and Darius was mindful enough to be receptive to it as well.

Lawrence, like most Good Samaritans, was observant, obedient, and optimistic in his approach. It would be such a shame to think of what might have resulted for Darius and his college life if Lawrence had been moseying around the midnight barbeque half engaged, splitting his attention with his cell phone and completely missing Darius walking by in the nine-tenths of his periphery outside his awareness. There's a chance that Darius and Lawrence would have continued to mindlessly walk by each other the following times as well since there wouldn't have been any established connection. Perhaps God would have sent someone else or He would have provided Lawrence with a second chance. The point is that we can never take for granted the opportunities we have in the moment because second chances are never a guarantee.

Discussion Questions and Tasks

1. In what ways have you experienced situational promptings in the past?
2. Share your results of the cell phone addiction assessment with others, and brainstorm ways in which you could get yourself to spend less time on your phone and more time interacting with others face-to-face or voice-to-voice.
3. Take a fifteen-minute tour and start up a conversation with at least one person along the way.

Chapter 5

Living Intentionally, Allowing for Spontaneity

*As Jesus and his disciples were on their way, he came to
a village where a woman named Martha opened her
home to him. She had a sister called Mary, who sat at the
Lord's feet listening to what he said. But Martha was
distracted by all the preparations that had to be made.
She came to him and asked, "Lord, don't you care that my
sister has left me to do the work by myself?
Tell her to help me!"
"Martha, Martha," the Lord answered, "you are
worried and upset about many things, but only one
thing is needed. Mary has chosen what is better, and
it will not be taken away from her."*

—Luke 10:38–42

In the Scripture above we see two lifestyles on display, both of which
we are quite familiar with. First, we have Martha who is diligent but emotionally unavailable. She gets the incredible opportunity to host Jesus
in her home, and she gets right to work to make sure every preparation
is taken care of and all things are in order. However, this comes at the

expense of emotionally neglecting her guest. Second, we have Mary who is attentive. She gets the same opportunity to host Jesus, and she loses sight of those preparations as she is fully focused on Jesus and hanging on His every word. In Mary's case, the preparations are neglected, but she and her guest are emotionally connected.

As a result, Jesus sets things straight as Martha's misplaced priorities are put on display for millions and millions of readers over the next couple thousand years. (Yikes, Martha really takes one for the team here.) Even worse, though, is that Jesus gives her the ole "Martha, Martha" rebuking. It's never a good sign when someone starts things off with the slow repeating of your name…

I don't know about you, but I have probably been in Martha's position far more often than I would like to admit. Too often I misplace my priorities in favor of tasks, to-dos, and preparations, completely losing sight of the uniquely wonderful people right in front of me. After I have done so, missing an opportunity for connection, I actually do feel the internal presence of God convicting me with the utterances of "Ryan, Ryan…" I'm just grateful that those mistakes, misplaced priorities, and miscalculations haven't been recorded in the world's most widely read book. After all, I once passively listened to my wife, giving her the generic "yeah" "um-hum" responses as I tried to block her out so that I could finish reading a marriage book chapter about turning toward instead of turning away from your spouse's emotional bids. Oh, the irony—what an idiot.

Martha and Mary's experience with Jesus is such a great example that highlights this idea of living intentionally and allowing for spontaneity. As it was mentioned in the preview to this section on Recognizing Divine Promptings, we all live busy lives these days. As a result, it would be foolish not to wake up with a game plan and a tentative schedule in place. The trick is being mindful enough, emotionally and spiritually, to recognize when a break from that schedule is needed. This may be one of the most important skills in need of development in the twenty-first century.

Living intentionally while allowing for spontaneity deals directly with this issue of how we lead productive *and* fulfilling lives. After all, this is essentially a culture clash between efficiency versus meaning. In the example of Martha and Mary, Mary was able to recognize this unique opportunity to have an intimate, meaningful conversation with Jesus Himself, so she broke free from focus on efficiency and allowed for some spontaneity by fully engaging with Jesus.

The tension of efficiency and meaning was made widely evident back in 2007 by a *Washington Post* experiment that went viral. I'm referring, of course, to the experiment and article by reporter Gene Weingarten.[30] Weingarten elicited the help of Joshua Bell, a world-class violinist and virtuoso, by having him dress in street clothes one January morning in a walkway outside a busy metro in downtown Washington, DC. Although Bell was dressed in street clothes, he was playing brilliantly complex classical pieces that few people on earth can play and doing so on a $3-million-dollar violin. On this particular morning, a little over a thousand people passed by Bell playing an instrument and music that people a few nights earlier were willing to pay hundreds of dollars to hear this same man play at Boston's Symphony Hall. However, this performance gained the attention of few, with only seven people stopping to fully engage for a few minutes and another twenty who threw change in his violin case but kept right on walking.

This experiment has since been a key piece of tangible evidence that is used to illustrate our ability to overlook astonishing people and performances amidst our "efficient," hurried venture through daily living. This is in large part due to the relational armor that we use to ward off outside influences. As mentioned in the chapter "Open Your Eyes to the Things Unseen," this relational armor could be made up of cell phones, sunglasses, ear buds, or other pieces of technology that highjack our attention away from our surroundings. As Weingarten stated in his article, "For many of us, the explosion of technology has perversely limited, not expanded, our exposure to new experiences."[31]

The relational armor could also be our to-do list and daily schedule, as these also have a way of highjacking our attention away from those around us. This is the more likely reason few people stopped to hear one of the world's greatest violinists. It is difficult to recognize someone as uniquely wonderful as Bell when he is out of context and we are in a rush, socially unavailable, and emotionally disengaged. The relational armor of a to-do list and preparation is the same reason that Martha missed an opportunity to connect with Jesus.

This experiment with Bell is a great reminder that God may be extending spiritual bids for our attention in less than obvious ways, which can easily fly under our radar. And if preoccupied and on the go, we may pass right by those very opportunities for life-giving and potentially life-altering conversations.

The following divine opportunity story from Tyler, a recent college graduate, highlights this notion of living intentionally and allowing for spontaneity, even when it comes at unexpected times. He writes:

To give you a little bit of backstory, I just graduated college and for the last couple of months I had been pursuing resident life positions in higher education for the coming fall. I had been looking at graduate programs at campuses across the country that would offer me a resident director position in the dorms working with undergraduates while I pursue a master's degree in higher education. I went to a conference for this particular area of interest in Oshkosh, Wisconsin, where I met with representatives from Mississippi State University. At the end of it all, they invited me for a second round of on-campus interviews. It was looking pretty good.

I went to Mississippi for the on-campus interview and had a great time and everything went really well. The only issue for me was that I had just spent the last two years at Azusa Pacific University in southern California surrounded by palm trees, beautiful weather, and a nearby ocean. And Mississippi is no California. The university is in the small town of Starkville, the ocean is not very close in comparison, and the nearest airport is two hours away. On the last morning of this trip to Mississippi, I was driving back to the airport and thinking, "I don't know if I can do this." I really enjoyed my trip and the people at the university, and I knew that God could use me there, but I was held back by the idea of spending two years in a remote town in a new part of the country where I didn't know anyone. On the drive to the airport, I received a phone call from the university telling me that I got the position and that they would love to have me there in the fall. I was feeling good about the position but hesitant about the overall move to Mississippi.

When I arrived at my gate at the airport I realized that my flights from Jackson to Dallas and from Dallas to LA had been cancelled for maintenance reasons. At this point, I was exhausted and ready to sleep, so I was kind of bummed that I had this major delay. But at the same time, I saw an elderly African-American man who was incredibly joyous and full of life, and he was chatting it up with everyone. His good mood was putting me in a better mood.

As I approached the desk to figure out how and when I was going to get back home, this man came over and introduced himself to me. He asked me what brought me to Mississippi, how I was doing, and what my passions were. I told him about the resident director position at the university and the purpose of my trip, and since he asked about my passion I gave him an honest reply. I told him that although I was excited about the position, my main passion was following Christ and I had a call on my life for men's ministry and working with men to help them truly live for Christ.

As I shared all of that, I looked at him and he just had the biggest smile on his face. He said, "I want you in my state. I'm going to be praying for you." I thanked him, and asked where he was traveling. He said that he was going to speak at Biola University, which is a Christian university near the one I attend in California. I asked him what his name was and what he was speaking about. He told me his name was John Perkins. And I just thought, "Holy smokes, this is stinkin' John Perkins!" I realize not everyone knows who that is, but this guy is a huge deal to me. If someone asked me if I could have dinner with any three people in the world, who would it be? John Perkins would be one of my three. He is the leader of church integration in the US, has had an amazing life living for Christ, and he has the most incredible life story. He is now eighty-four years old, and more joyous and happy than anyone I've ever met.

As it turned out, we were on the same flights for the rest of the day, which were significantly delayed. I decided to grab a table to get something to eat and invited him and his assistant to join me for lunch. I got to pray for John Perkins's meal! I was able to sit and talk with him for an hour and half to two hours. John Perkins sat and talked with me about ministry and grace the whole time. Toward the end of our conversation, he said to me, "Tyler, if I'm still living when you get to Mississippi, I want to come alongside you and do ministry with you." To me that's like a superhero saying that he wants to work with me. I was just like, "God, what are You doing?" It was incredible. It was as if God sent His servant John to intervene in my trip, to speak truth to me, and encourage me about being in Mississippi for a reason.

I left that feeling like, "Yeah, I have a lot of fears, but I'm not going to shy away from what God is doing here." I went from just wanting to sleep on an airplane to meeting John Perkins and having the most amazing conversation. Honestly, if the flights hadn't been delayed, and the flight plan would have carried out as normal, I probably would have got right on the flight and immediately fallen asleep. I was so tired and ready to get back home that I don't think I would have ever recognized him or had a conversation with him. And now I'm happy to tell you that I have officially decided to move to Mississippi and take on this new adventure.

I love how God paired these two together on Tyler's trip. It's so fun to hear a story from a recent college graduate who is so spiritually mature and open to God's guidance. Tyler and John's opportunity and interaction is a perfect example of what it means to be living intentionally while allowing for spontaneity. In fact, it reminds me of the following Scripture:

> As Jesus was walking beside the Sea of Galilee, he saw two brothers, Simon called Peter and his brother Andrew. They were casting a net into the lake, for they were fishermen. "Come, follow me," Jesus said, "and I will make you fishers of men." At once they left their nets and followed him. (Matthew 4:18–20)

With Tyler, it was as if he was finishing up his trip, preparing for a new career, and doubting his move to Mississippi, when along came John Perkins, who, on behalf of God, said to Tyler, "Come, follow Me." And just like that, Tyler left his worries behind and followed Him.

Emotional and Spiritual Approachability, Availability, Agility

Both Tyler and John displayed the three essential characteristics for living intentionally and allowing for spontaneity, which includes emotional and spiritual approachability, availability, and agility. If you want to live intentionally and allow for spontaneity, spend some time reflecting upon these concepts and what they mean for you in your life.

Approachability

Approachability includes the nonverbal communication cues that we are sending out to others through our eye contact or lack thereof, facial expressions, body posture, gestures, clothing, and accessories. All of these nonverbal aspects have implications as to whether someone is more or less likely to approach us in conversation or whether we are more or less likely to approach others in conversation. The next time you are out in public take a moment and look at the various people around you. Do a quick assessment of the people you would be more likely to engage with versus the people you would be more likely to avoid. Odds are that you can quickly, consciously and subconsciously, identify aspects of the person's nonverbal cues that make them more or less approachable. The same is true for when others are looking at you.

This exercise has increased my awareness significantly, which is why I try to be mindful of my approachability when I'm out in public. I have a few things going for me and a few things going against me. On the approachable side of things, I am somewhat clean cut, tall, lanky, and I have a small head. That may seem a bit random, but there have been several occasions when I've been in a group of people and strangers will wander over to me to ask a general question that they could have asked anyone around me. I think that has a lot to do with the fact that I generally try to keep my head up, a slight smile on my face, and the fact that I'm 6' 4" with a small head certainly doesn't hurt either. The height helps me to stand out in a crowd and the small head makes me look quite innocent and unintimidating. Having a small head has been annoying when it comes to picking out sunglasses and hats, but it's all part of my God-given nonthreatening design. In fact, I was once in an elevator with two African-American middle-aged women, and after a few seconds one of them turned to me and said, "You just have the cutest little head." I took it as a compliment and it turned into a conversation.

On the unapproachable side of things, I can be quite shy around strangers and people I don't know very well. As a result, I think that my shyness and reserved nature can be taken as standoffish and potentially be interpreted as me being too cool for school. This is certainly an area for growth and mindfulness. We all have pros and cons when it comes to approachability and others' willingness to engage with us in conversation.

In a recent research methods class that I teach, we sent out a survey to 204 participants and one of the questions we asked was, "Which nonverbal cues would most likely keep you from starting a conversation with someone? Check all that apply." Here are the results:

"they look like they are in a hurry" at 60 percent (122 out of 205)
"they have headphones in their ears" at 57 percent (117 out of 205)
"their head is down looking at their cell phone" at 40 percent (82 out of 204)
"they look like they are in a bad mood" at 37 percent (75 out of 204)

This is vitally important for us to be mindful of, because one or more of these cues could diminish our approachability and lead to a missed opportunity for a great conversation with someone. Each of these is a part of the relational armor that keeps people at bay as we wander through our day. In fact, I regularly see people display all of these. A huge percentage of the population is regularly in a hurry, looking at their cell phone, listening to music through their ear buds, and to top it all off they may even have a little bit of a frump-face going on, giving the impression that they are in a bad mood.

As we think back to Tyler's description of John Perkins, we get a great picture of someone who was incredibly approachable. John was smiling, walking around, and just had an all-around joyful presence about him. My father-in-law, David, mentioned in the earlier chapters, is just like John Perkins. If you bump into him in public you can't help but smile and appreciate his positivity and joy. These guys' joy legitimately comes from their relationship and love for God and genuine appreciation for life. It's fun to see and experience, and it's very contagious.

That's the way every Christian should be. Our love for God and appreciation for life ought to shine through in our approachability toward others. Sing it with me, "This little light of mine, I'm gonna let it shine, let it shine, let it shine, let it shine. Hide it behind an iPhone, no! I'm gonna let it shine. Hide it behind a frumpy-face, no! I'm gonna let it shine. Hide it behind a to-do list, no! I'm gonna let it shine, let it shine, let it shine, let it shine."

Availability

After approachability, the next element of living intentionally and allowing for spontaneity in conversation involves our emotional availability, which, for even the top percentage of people, those Triple O Christians who are observant, obedient, and optimistic, is potentially lower than you might think. Dr. John Gottman, the world's leading relationship expert, helps us understand why that might be. Below is how Dr. Gottman describes two people's emotional availability and likelihood for emotional connection:

> If you were to estimate the percentage of time you are with your partner that you are emotionally available, ready to listen non-defensively, with an open heart, with empathy, would you agree that 50% is a generous estimate? Most people I've asked would agree. That's the probability of getting a heads by flipping an unbiased coin.
>
> Now ask the question, "What's the probability that both partners will be emotionally available at the same time?" Assuming independence, that probability

is the same as flipping two coins and getting two heads, which is 25%. Therefore, even with that generous estimate, 75% of the time is ripe ground for miscommunication, a regrettable incident, and [a missed opportunity]. If we used a more conservative estimate of 30% emotional availability, 91% would become ripe ground for miscommunication.[32]

Thinking about emotional and spiritual availability in those terms always puts things into perspective. This means that from the moment we wake up to the moment we go to bed, 75 to 91 percent of our daily interactions are ripe ground for miscommunication and missed opportunities. You might think that estimate seems too high for your liking. This estimate accounts for the fact that *both* people in conversation need to be emotionally available and emotionally engaged *at the same time*. In order for both people to be emotionally engaged, this means that *both* people must be simultaneously ready to listen non-defensively, with an open heart, and with empathy, and *neither* person is likely to be hungry, tired, distracted, busy, preoccupied, physically fatigued, mentally fatigued, angry, upset, or in a foul mood. When we think about our emotional and spiritual availability in those terms, it is easy to understand why the vast amount of our day is subject to feeling like an interruption rather than an opportunity.

This is an area that I struggle with myself. I have two small children, ages three and a half and one and a half, and a more than full-time job. So I'm not getting a ton of sleep these days and I am regularly tired. Unfortunately, this physical exhaustion keeps me from making the most of many opportunities throughout the course of the week. In fact, just this morning my sweet little princess vomited all over me before I was getting ready to leave for work. What a great way to start the day! This is just one reason why it's important for me to continue to find ways to refocus and reenergize so that I don't let this exhaustion rob me of divine opportunities.

Hunger is another emotionally draining variable for me. I'm hypoglycemic, so when I get hungry I am 100 percent worthless. I can't focus, I get tunnel vision, and I just zone out. I try to stay on top of this so it doesn't rob me of conversation, which is why I have to eat dinner before I go to dinner parties. If I show up hungry I can't enjoy any of the conversation before we get around to eating. This is why all my friends think I don't eat very much, because by the time I eat with them I'm already on my second dinner.

When it comes to emotional availability, self-awareness and self-management is key. If you aren't already, you should become intimately familiar with what your availability shortcomings are and how you can avoid those personal pitfalls and tendencies. This is why whenever I start to act a little short or disconnected, my wife will tell me to go and eat something. We are both aware of my barriers to emotional availability and try to be proactive whenever possible.

What are your availability barriers—hunger, physical exhaustion, emotional exhaustion, hurried, preoccupied, technologically distracted? What ways can you be proactive to avoid your own personal availability pitfalls? These are important questions to consider so that we can make ourselves as emotionally available to others as possible and decrease the percentage of times that would otherwise be ripe for miscommunication and missed opportunities. Let's strive to increase the percentage of time we are emotionally available, ready to listen nondefensively, with an open heart, and with empathy.

Agility

The third aspect to living intentionally and allowing for spontaneity is one's emotional agility. Emotional agility deals with how open you are to accepting the influence of others. As stated in Romans 12:15, "Rejoice with those who rejoice; mourn with those who mourn." In this case, flexibility, adaptability, and emotional mobility are essential to living intentionally and allowing for spontaneity. As Gottman has discovered, masters in relationships have significantly less emotional inertia than do disasters in relationships. In fact, "Happiness, in love seems to mean that they are each 'lighter,' and less immovable during [conversation]."[33] Ultimately, those who are emotionally agile are adaptable to the momentary needs of others, and they are capable of being moved emotionally in one direction or another to acclimate to their conversational partner.

This can also be traced back to Tyler and John Perkins's divine opportunity. Tyler commented, "At this point, I'm just so exhausted and ready to sleep, so I was kind of bummed that I had this major delay. But at this same time, I see an elderly African-American man who is so joyous and full of life, and he is chatting it up with everyone. So his good mood was putting me in a better mood." In this case, John was able to positively influence Tyler's attitude, which snapped Tyler out of his tired funk and woke him up emotionally and spiritually to the ensuing divine opportunity. Think ut the ripple effect of John Perkins's joyous attitude and enthusiasm for life. This is just one story from Tyler. I'm sure there are thousands of other people who have caught a whiff of John's joy and been emotionally transformed in the process.

The objective here is not to avoid negative feelings at all cost and simply put on a happy face despite all that may be going on. As a couple of leadership consultants have noted, "Leaders stumble not because they *have* undesirable thoughts and feelings—that's inevitable—but because they get *hooked* by them, like fish caught on a line."[34] Again, Tyler could have easily been hooked and caught up by his exhaustion, but instead he allowed himself to be brought out of that mood by the spirit, energy, and interest of John.

Below is a divine opportunity shared by Georgia, a seventy-five-year-old woman, who, along with two others, exhibits this lifestyle of living intentionally while allowing for spontaneity. In the course of her story, we can see moments of approachability, availability, and agility.

> About a year ago, I randomly decided to stay home from work while my husband was at a doctor's appointment. I didn't have any specific reason to stay home from work that day; I just had an urge to do so. On this particular day, a gentleman from the electric company came to read the electric meter. When this man arrived, he walked around to the back of the house to read the meter. While he was back there, he saw my husband's old John Deere bulldozer. When he was finished reading the meter, he came back around to the front and knocked on the door. He excitedly asked about the bulldozer and who it belonged to. I told him that it was my husband's and that he planned to fix it up and get it working again. However, he had since contracted terminal cancer and was unable to do any work on it at this point. This gentleman asked me to check with my husband to see if he could come over and help him work on it and get it running again. I told him I would ask my husband for him when he got back home.
>
> When my husband returned from his doctor's appointment, I told him about the man who was reading the meter and asked about helping him fix up the bulldozer. My husband turned to me and said, "You and your prayers!" Meeting this man was a divine opportunity, because I had no idea what I was going to do with that bulldozer in my backyard knowing my husband was dying and that he couldn't do anything about fixing it up or trying to move it. This man was truly an answer to our prayers.

This gentleman wasn't getting paid and didn't even have much experience fixing this kind of machinery. He just had a desire to learn about the mechanics of it from my husband and have a chance to fix up an old bulldozer.

Sure enough, my husband and this man talked and worked out a schedule for the two of them to regularly meet and work on the bulldozer. For weeks, the two of them would be in the back working on this project in the evenings and on the weekends. My husband would instruct him what to do and he would do it. It wasn't too long before they had it back up and running again.

Interestingly, while this gentleman was over working on one of those days, he shared with us that the day he came to read our meter was actually the first time he had been out of the office to do so. He had never been on a meter read before. He was from the main office and that day he just had a feeling to take the meter reader's place, and go and try out the whole thing. He really didn't even belong there that day. Similarly, I shouldn't have been home that day either. I should have been at work myself. And my husband was away at his doctor's appointment, so under normal circumstances the three of us would have never crossed paths.

After they finished the work on the bulldozer, I was taking my husband to the hospital for another appointment. On the way to the hospital, I saw this huge truck that hauled big equipment off on the side of the road. I immediately had a strong feeling to stop and talk to the man who was standing by the truck. After feeling this urge, I pulled over, got out, told him about my husband's health situation and the bulldozer, and asked him if he might be able to move it for us. To my surprise, he immediately said, "Of course, I would be happy to do that. When and where do you want it moved?" I just couldn't believe how easy it was, and how responsive and open he was to the whole idea.

This man came over to our house the next week to load and move the bulldozer. He initially tried to help my husband up into the bulldozer so he could be the one to drive it onto his hauler, but my husband was in too bad of shape to get up there. He eventually jumped in the bulldozer, drove it around to the front, loaded it up on his hauler, and got it ready to move. When we asked this man why he was being so kind and generous—because this was a significant amount of time, effort, and expense—he said that he was doing all this in honor of his father who had died. By helping my husband, it was a way of giving back in his father's name. It was a touching and special moment. Then minutes later he hauled it off and was gone just like that.

Meeting both of those gentleman were divine opportunities—again, I had no idea what I was going to do with that bulldozer knowing my husband was dying. I had never seen these two men before and I have never seen them since. The Lord worked it all out perfectly. When the Lord moves it's always at the right time—never too early and never too late. This taught me the lesson to wait on the Lord and not get ahead of what He can do for us.

What an incredible story of three different people living intentionally, allowing for spontaneity through emotional and spiritual approachability, availability, and agility. All three of these people—Georgia, the meter reader, and the hauler—had jobs to do and work that needed to be done. Yet each of them allowed for a spontaneous prompting and nudging to take priority over their typical daily activity. What resulted was not only incredibly powerful for Georgia and her husband, but it seems like these other two men also experienced the fulfillment of a longing themselves. After all, the meter reader was awfully eager to learn the mechanics of the bulldozer and the hauler was responding on behalf of his own father. It would be fun to hear this story from their perspectives as well. But that's all part of the mystery of divine opportunities.

Discussion Questions

1. What are your approachability and availability barriers—hunger, physical exhaustion, emotional exhaustion, hurried, preoccupied, technologically distracted?
2. Ask your friends and family what seem to be your barriers to appearing approachable and being emotionally available?
3. In what ways can you be proactive to avoid your own personal approachability and availability pitfalls?

Part Two

Taking Conversational Risks

The first section of this book, Recognizing Divine Opportunities, was all about opening our eyes and ears to the spiritual and situational promptings that are all around us and making ourselves available amidst a balancing act of living intentionally while allowing for spontaneity. This next section is about preparing ourselves to take conversational risks. One of the themes in the interviews I conducted with divine opportunities was this notion of risk taking. Whether it is large or small, each divine opportunity required the person to overcome momentary fears, worries, or concerns in order to initiate a conversation, share something personal, or turn a conversation toward a difficult or sensitive topic.

The Christians who have the types of the divine experiences and stories you have read thus far do so because they took a step out in faith that perhaps others wouldn't have taken. The number one reason people miss opportunities is because of their own fears and anxieties about what may follow. The ultimate source of these fears is the potential for social rejection. "Social rejection—or fearing it—is one of the most common causes of anxiety."[35] Being rejected, ignored, or disregarded in conversation can carry with it a particularly harsh social sting. The potential for social rejection is often enough to derail people from being obedient to a prompt God. However, there was something about these Triple O (observ dient, optimistic) Christians who experienced these same fears but decided to lean into those fears and take a social risk in order to find out where God was leading them in the moment.

Wayne Gretzky, the Hall of Fame hockey player, said it best, "You miss 100 percent of the shots you don't take." This quote applies wonderfully to divine opportunities. We all need to spend some quality time exploring our own personal experiences with divine opportunities and missed opportunities, and what this means for our faith, belief, and trust in God. Of course, God doesn't promise us that we will make 100 percent of the shots we take, but that's all part of the adventure. In fact, even the Triple O Christians will tell you that they don't always experience the types of outcomes as exhibited in the stories in this book. This is because not all divine opportunities are going to be monumental experiences, transforming conversations, or course-correcting interactions. More often than not, divine opportunities may just have the slightest of recognizable influence. They might not even have any recognizable influence at all for us on this side of heaven.

The motivation that we need to keep in mind is that our willingness to recognize promptings, overcome fears, and engage others in conversation is all about "loving regardless of results."[36] Going out on a relational limb and taking a risk is ultimately an act of worship. It's a way of letting God know that you are willing to love others around you by engaging them in conversation regardless of the results—big, small, or seemingly none at all.

The focus of these chapters is based on this simple observation: I am yet to hear a story about a time when someone felt a prompting, recognized an opportunity, engaged someone in conversation, and that person went on to deeply regret doing so. However, I have heard plenty of stories from people who felt a prompting, recognized an opportunity, and failed to engage someone in conversation, and greatly regretted doing so. The long-term regret from a missed opportunity is far more painful than the short-term social sting from following up on a prompting and being ignored or disregarded in conversation.

This section will explore the most common conversational barriers people experience, how to identify key turning points in conversation, and how to navigate those stress-inducing turning points with optimistic obedience.

Chapter 6

Conversational Barriers

*Moses said to the L*ORD, *"O Lord, I have never been eloquent, neither in the past nor since you have spoken to your servant. I am slow of speech and tongue." The L*ORD *said to him, "Who gave man his mouth? Who makes him deaf or mute? Who gives him sight or makes him blind? Is it not I, the L*ORD? *Now go; I will help you speak and will teach you what to say." But Moses said, "O Lord, please send someone else to do it."*

—Exodus 4:10–13

Here we have one of the key, pivotal biblical leaders in history expressing such incredible self-doubt. When Moses was approached by God to lead His people out of slavery in Egypt and into the Promised Land, he begged God to use someone else. Moses's barrier was his lack of communication confidence and competence. If you read on in the story of Moses, he essentially said to God, "How about You use my bro, Aaron? Dude can really lay down some serious chitter chatter; Aaron has a real way with people and a way with words. He kills it on the Scrabble table as well as on the speed dating circuit. He's the triple-threat kind of guy You're looking for; not me." (Some culturally relevant liberties have been taken here.)

Moses had the hardest time getting past these fears, worries, and concerns. Yet, as readers, we can now look at his situation and think, "Boy, was that silly—that's so ridiculous that Moses of all people would be fearful and hesitant. God appeared to him in a burning bush and then he is going to doubt God's ability to use him as a leader?" But we have the luxury of a retrospective view, knowing how things turned out for Moses. The same can be said for us. I'm sure there are plenty of times each of us have been fearful and hesitant to take a risk, engage a difficult conversation, and stretch our comfort zones, yet if we had a long-term retrospective view we would realize how ridiculous those fears were in comparison to how things actually played out.

Do you understand the irony of our fears, worries, and concerns when it comes to responding to God's promptings in initiating conversations with others? Take me for example. From twenty-one to twenty-four years of age I regularly performed stand-up comedy, putting myself out there by my lonesome on a stage where it's do or die. At twenty-three, I loaded up my Mazda Millenia and moved from Kansas City to Hollywood without an apartment, job, or any security. At twenty-five, I went skydiving and jumped out of a plane at 10,000 feet. And yet somehow I can still manage to be nervous about walking across a room, introducing myself to a stranger, and striking up a conversation. How completely backward is that?

One of the keys to engaging in divine opportunities is understanding our unique and individual emotional profiles and barriers to conversation. Our emotional profile essentially gets at "how well we can control what we do and say and feel during an emotional episode."[37] Part of your emotional profile is comprised of your emotional triggers, which are influenced by your personal experiences of the past as well as your cultural and familial upbringing.[38] Your culture, family, and personal experiences all influence what triggers your emotional responses of fears, worries, concerns, and joys. These emotional triggers and your behavioral responses can be the difference between engaging in or missing a divine opportunity.

As an example of the negative side to these emotional triggers, conversational barriers, and responses of flight rather than fight, I've included the following missed opportunity. This missed opportunity for a divine conversation comes from Jean, a fifty-nine-year-old marketing manager.

> My missed opportunity involved my dad. But before I get too far into the story, you should get this mental picture of him. My dad was kind of a Mr. Party guy—he loved to party. He was

pretty self-centered when you boil it all down. He was about 6'2", always been an outdoorsman or sports guy, a big guy with rough hands, and a big cowboy belt with a big buckle and boots—that sort of thing. You never wanted to cross my dad. Even as an adult I didn't want to cross him, make him angry, or have him be upset with me. His whole life he always made it a point that he never wanted anything to do with religion and all "those kinds of people." He was busy doing his own thing and so that would have interfered with his lifestyle. My mom and dad divorced years ago and I didn't see much of him. You know, every girl wants to have a close relationship with her dad, and I never felt like I had that.

Well, we finally reconnected in '95 or '96, so every year I'd take my vacation and we'd go see my dad over his birthday. Our relationship began to get a bit stronger, but there was never a real close bond. In 2002, he was living in Tennessee, down on a river where he had built himself this little house. His health had gotten really bad. His arthritis had gotten so bad that he couldn't get up and down the steps and do the things that he liked to do. As I was visiting with him this particular week, he shared with me that he felt like he needed to go live some place with assistance, and that his sister had actually invited him to live with her. So he took her up on the offer, and decided he was going to liquidate everything to be able to make the move.

At the end of the week, I told him that I'd come back and help him pack. So I went home, got my stuff together, and came back to spend two weeks helping him liquidate everything. We spent all that time together and I felt like we were getting a little bit closer. Then on the morning that I was getting ready to leave, I woke up in the early hours with a sense, this feeling that I needed to talk to him—I needed to tell him about the Lord. It was the intense urging. I mean I was laying there that morning, I was scripting everything that I would say, but at the same time I couldn't do it. I had the strongest feeling and urge in my spirit, but my body and mind were resisting. There was just no doubt what God was prompting me to do, and I was really rebelling.

I didn't want to upset my dad and didn't want him mad at me. I was just lying there saying to God, "I know You want me to talk to him, but I know Dad and I don't want to hurt him, I don't want to offend him, I don't want him mad at me." So I was fighting with myself, and I guess with God too, because He was clearly telling me to do it.

Anyway, I got up and I went and sat down at the dining room table and visited with him. Finally my dad said, "You seem a little upset, what's wrong?" And I just sort of lied, "Oh, I'm just upset that I don't have everything done for you, and I'm going to have to leave today." And he said, "You've helped me so much— don't worry about it, I appreciate it." But I didn't tell him that I was feeling led to tell him about the Lord. I had every opportunity, because that very morning he was looking for Charles Stanley, the pastor, on TV. Apparently, he had been watching him over the past year or so and he wanted to hear Charles Stanley and he couldn't find it on the TV that morning. That should have been an open door for me to talk to him, but I just couldn't bring myself to do it. Finally, I reached a point where I had to leave, because it was a long drive home, so we said our goodbyes and I went home.

It was obvious he wanted to talk about something or do something that day. Whether it would have been leading him to the Lord or just speaking to him in some other way, I don't know. I believe that he would have been receptive that day because of the intensity of the drawing of the Spirit to talk to him and since he was trying to find Charles Stanley on TV that morning. That should have been an open door of opportunity and I just didn't take it. But I have to believe that he would have been receptive.

I wish I had been able to let him know how wonderful God is, let him know that God wanted to be a part of his life, show him how awesome He was, and try to build a relationship between him and God. Basically, I wish I had been able to witness to him about what God had done in me and through me, and how He'd impacted my life. Instead, it was just normal chitchat, really nothing of any significance at all. Just talking about his move and what he was going to do and that kind of thing.

The following weekend my aunt and uncle came down and picked up my dad. They packed up his stuff in the trailer and went home. Three weeks to the day, my dad got up on a Saturday morning, extremely bloated, and in an extreme amount of pain, and before the day was over he died. We think he probably had an aneurism in his stomach, but we don't know for sure. But the point is that I never had a chance to witness to him, share about the Lord, and ask him about his relationship with God. And now I will never know whether or not my dad had ever decided to accept Jesus. I will never know where my dad is spending eternity.

> I've thought about the conversation or the lack of conversation and the missed opportunity many times since that day. I don't know for sure what would have resulted because the conversation didn't happen. He died and I don't know whether he was saved, I don't know where he stood with God, and maybe it would have just been the peace of mind for me and my aunt and family if we had just known. It's a reminder that we need to do what God calls us to do. I know God doesn't love me any less, and I still love Him, but it's a sad occurrence that happens in life. We never know what tomorrow holds and we never should question God, because there is a reason and purpose for all those promptings and opportunities.

What a difficult missed opportunity. Based on my own experiences and conversations and interviews with others, Jean's missed opportunity really is not that unique in terms of the prompting to raise a difficult topic, share something personal, and take a little bit of relational risk. What makes her experience unique is the untimely nature of her father's passing, which made this missed opportunity so much more impactful, memorable, and unfortunate.

I pray that we all learn a lesson from the missed opportunity from Jean as well as our own past missed opportunities. The goal is to train ourselves in the ways of the Lord so that we can miss fewer opportunities and engage in more divine appointments. The good news is that there are some practical steps that we can all take to improve our ability to understand our unique emotional profiles, triggers, patterns, thoughts, and emotions so that we can move toward recognition and acceptance of those triggers and respond in conversation based on our Christian values rather than our fears.

Acceptance and Commitment Therapy

Acceptance and Commitment Therapy is a form of behavioral analysis that allows people to thoughtfully and mindfully evaluate their thoughts, feelings, and emotions, label those emotions, accept those emotions for what they are, and in turn act on their values. The ultimate goal is to move away from fear-evoked reactions and move toward value-based responses.

The four particular strategies that will be outlined here are from David and Congleton,[39] who modified the original therapy techniques from psychologist Steven Hayes. The following four strategies can assist us all in getting unhooked by our emotions so that we can live a life of observation, obedience, and optimism rather than regret, what-ifs, and missed opportunities. The key is to learn to give ourselves some time to reflect on our values and priorities in between our initial emotional trigger and our response to others.

Recognize Your Patterns

"By noticing certain telltale signs, you'll start to realize where you're getting stuck."[40] Recognizing patterns requires us to thoughtfully consider a variety of people, topics, and situations and environments that elicit particular thoughts and feelings.

People patterns. As far as people are concerned, everyone has their unique cast of characters that elicit both positive and negative emotions inside of us. We all can think of those individuals who immediately make us feel fearful, self-doubting, or defensive. This was the case for Jean and the emotional patterns that had been established with her dad. So when the opportunity presented itself for her to share with him about her faith and inquire about his, she slipped right into the established pattern of emotion. In her case, this led to self-doubt, timidity, and the fear of upsetting him. Jean is certainly not alone in this. Who are the people or types of people you have difficulty engaging in conversation? Why and what can you learn from recognizing these people patterns?

Topical patterns. The same goes for recognizing common and recurring topics that trigger a variety of emotions, both positive and negative. For example, you might be completely comfortable making small talk with people and talking about general interests, but when it comes to talking about faith, politics, sexuality, or Northern Ireland you may quickly get apprehensive, anxious, and nervous. This can also be noted in Jean's story as well, as she described how she had spent two weeks with her dad and was growing closer in the process. Clearly she had no problem making small talk and having regular conversation with her dad the first thirteen days of her two-week trip. Then, on the last day of the trip, the one time it came for her to raise the topic of faith, she froze up and could not bring herself to even mention it at all.

I regret to say that I am no better than Jean. I can talk all day long about faith with other people whom I know are Christians, but if I bump into someone who isn't a Christian I am very hesitant to bring up the subject. Shoot, I'll start saying words that rhyme with "Jesus" and see how they react to those words first before I slowly try to muster up some courage to move into a riskier domain. What topics do you have difficulty discussing with others? Why and what can you learn from recognizing these topical patterns?

Situational and environmental patterns. One of the most common barriers to divine opportunities that I have come across is what I call "situational perfectionism." This is when people find themselves rationalizing their disobedience to God's prompting by saying it was "poor timing." I'll just wait for a better time, a more private place, or a more comfortable situation to have the conversation. It is easy for people to miss opportunities because they are quick to say that the timing isn't quite right, or there were too many distractions, or they had pink eye. The point is that some situational and environmental excuses are warranted while other times we may just be looking for any excuse to justify our disobedience to God's promptings.

This is the equivalent of the Goldilocks effect, when Goldilocks commits a misdemeanor and does a little B&E (breaking and entering for those of you who aren't down with the street lingo), and barges into the home of the three bears. She starts to eat their soup but complains about it being too hot, then too cold, before she finally finds the third bowl to be just right. Do you tend to recognize this Goldilocks effect in your delay and rationalizing of the situational perfectionism when opportunities present themselves in everyday life?

This is important to consider, within reason. I understand that some conversations are better suited for private versus public settings. Sometimes people can be in a rush with one foot out of the conversation and it's not a good time to get vulnerable. But you certainly don't want to pass on an opportunity because the conditions weren't exactly perfect, because the conditions you were presented with might just be as good as it's going to get. And, like Jean said, you never know what tomorrow holds or if you will ever get a second chance. What types of situational or environmental patterns make it more or less likely that you will engage someone in conversation? Why are you impacted by certain situational factors and what can you learn from identifying these patterns?

Label Your Thoughts and Emotions

"Labeling allows you to see your thoughts and feelings for what they are: transient sources of information that may or may not prove helpful."[41] I have found that in both missed opportunities and fulfilled divine opportunities, people will always experience some level of emotional laden hesitancy, which results in a conversational barrier. These conversational barriers cause people to second-guess the spiritual or situational promptings, and lead them to question whether or not they should engage the other person in conversation at all. The difference between the missed opportunity and divine opportunity stories was that during the missed opportunities these barriers would keep people from fully engaging the other person and ultimately led them in the direction of disobedience and inaction. In the divine opportunity stories, the barriers simply delayed the obedient action as people eventually took a relational risk and moved forward.

Here is a list of the most common conversational barriers (thoughts, feelings, and emotions) that were evident in people's stories. Take a look at the list and identify which of these barriers most resonate with you personally.

Fear of conflict, embarrassment, criticism, rejection, judgment, or being considered a "Jesus Freak."
Not in tune with God.
Situational perfectionism.
Caught off guard by the opportunity.
Opportunity was inconvenient (poor timing).
Anxious or nervous.
Too busy.
Lack of communication confidence.
Lack of urgency.
Awkwardness.
Skepticism of the promptings.
Underestimating God.
Insecure.
Pessimistic attitude about the outcome.
Physically exhausted.
Emotionally exhausted.

This is all about you figuring out your own personal and unique emotional profile. Which thoughts and emotions have the biggest impact on you personally when it comes to what you will or will not say and do in conversation? This is an incredibly important step for increasing your own self-awareness, labeling your thoughts and emotions, and taking action to overcome these emotions.

Name it to tame it, baby. I love this line, "Name it to tame it." Feel the power in that statement. This is the act of moving from self-awareness to self-management. The main purpose here is to recognize the most common negative, self-defeating thoughts, feelings, and emotions you experience personally. Once you name these feelings, then you can begin to anticipate them before they even arise; this way the emotions won't catch you off guard. You can say to yourself, "I'm sensing a spiritual or situational prompting, I'm noticing an opportunity here, and I know that I am about to feel the fear of rejection, the fear of judgment, and overall insecurity." Which is usually followed by, "Yep, there they all are; just as anticipated." You may even feel your heart rate increase, you may start to sweat a bit, and feel some butterflies in your stomach. If you take the time to identify and anticipate these feelings, they will no longer take you by surprise, and instead you will be in a position to tame those feelings.

Accept Your Thoughts and Feelings for What They Are

"Respond to your ideas and emotions with an open attitude, pay attention to them, and let yourself experience them."[42] These fears, worries, and concerns are nothing to be embarrassed about; they are completely normal. Nearly everyone experiences these similar emotions and thoughts to varying degrees. The key is to be mindful of these thoughts and feelings, allow yourself to take them in stride, and then seek to control those emotions rather than allow them to control you. God said through Isaiah:

> So do not fear, for I am with you; do not be dismayed, for I am your God. I will strengthen you and help you; I will uphold you with my righteous right hand…. For I am the Lord, your God, who takes hold of your right hand and says to you, Do not fear; I will help you. (Isaiah 41:10,13)

Then in 2 Chronicles 20:15,17, it says:

> This is what the Lord says to you: 'Do not be afraid or discouraged because of this vast army. For the battle is not yours, but God's…. You will not have to fight this battle. Take up your positions; stand firm and see the deliverance the Lord will give you."

Do not forget that as Christians we possess the ultimate secret weapon, the Trinity—the Father, the Son, and the Holy Spirit. This is the most incredible emotion-controlling superpower anyone could ask for. When it comes to accepting and moving forward despite these fears, worries, and concerns, we have direct access to a God who will hold us up under any condition. When you experience these conversational barriers, recognize them, label them, and then tame them by turning them over to God. After all, those defeating thoughts and feelings that you are experiencing may just be spiritual warfare, which is trying to take hold of you in order to keep you from experiencing something transformational. And the antidote to spiritual warfare is turning lose the power of the name of Jesus. Jesus is the ultimate fear-tamer, for He said in John 16:23–24:

> In that day you will no longer ask me anything. I tell you the truth, my Father will give you whatever you ask in my name. Until now you have not asked for anything in my name. Ask and you will receive, and your joy will be complete.

Act on Your Values

"You can decide to act in a way that aligns with your values when you unhook yourself from difficult thoughts and emotions."[43] Once you have recognized your patterns, labeled your thoughts and emotions, accepted them for what they are, now it is time to intervene in the moment and choose to act on your values. David and Congleton offer several great questions for leaders to consider in the passing moment between stimulus and response to help guide them toward a value-based decision and action. I've modified them a bit here:[44]

- Is your response to God's promptings and your initial emotional reaction going to serve you and the other person in the long term as well as in the short term?
- Will your response help you steer others in a direction that furthers your collective purpose?
- Are you taking a step closer to being the Christian you most want to be and living the Christian life you most want to live?

The following quote is a great reminder why this four-step process of Acceptance and Commitment Therapy is so important: "The mind's thought stream flows endlessly, and emotions change like the weather, but values can be called on at any time, in any situation."[45] Variations of this form of behavioral analysis have been supported with evidence of effectiveness, and I can't help but think just how much more effective it could be by calling on the Father, the Son, and the Holy Spirit in the midst of it all.

Paul reminds us:

> So I say, live by the Spirit, and you will not gratify the desires of the sinful nature. For the sinful nature desires what is contrary to the Spirit, and the Spirit what is contrary to the sinful nature. They are in conflict with each other, so that you do not do what you want. But if you are led by the Spirit, you are not under the law. (Galatians 5:16–18)

To close out this chapter on overcoming the conversational barriers amidst divine opportunities, I would like to share with you a divine appointment from Kelsey, a twenty-seven-year-old youth ministry volunteer. Kelsey, without knowing, applies many of these strategies for acceptance and commitment to overcome her initial barriers, fears, worries, and concerns to engage in a life-changing interaction. She says:

> The summer before my senior year of high school I went on a mission trip to Mexico with my youth group. We were paired up with a team of Mexican Christians and we were doing mime work on the streets of Mexico. We would present a drama in Spanish and then the Mexicans would present the gospel in Spanish. Then they would invite the people in the town who were out on the streets to come up for prayer.
>
> I was young and kind of insecure, not with my faith but being bold about my faith. And I wasn't comfortable with jumping out and initiating anything at that time. When these moments of prayer would come around, I would wait for someone else who spoke Spanish to go pray for somebody, and then I would follow behind. I usually wouldn't pray because in my little feeble mind at that time, I thought, "Well, they can't understand me anyway. So I'll just pray internally while others pray in their language."
>
> I never initiated any prayer and I didn't pray out loud until this one particular day. It was the end of the day, late afternoon, and we were out in the middle of this big open shopping plaza area. There were probably sixty to eighty Mexican people gathered around, and they had listened to the drama and then we'd given an altar call. For whatever reason, it was really busy that day with people coming forward. I just remember passively following people around to pray off in the wings while others took the lead. Then I started to realize that there weren't enough

people to pray for the ones who were coming forward. So I felt like the Lord was encouraging me to kind of take my blinders off and pursue someone.

At that time, there was a little older lady over to my left, and she was standing away from everyone else, and she wasn't even asking for prayer. But she was standing there and she was just weeping. I remember her making eye contact with me but looking very hesitant and scared. She just looked at me like, "I'm here. This is as far as I can come. Will you meet me halfway?" I remember God, like a beam of light was telling me, "Go to her."

Initially, I was in denial. Looking at her, knowing that God was telling me to go over there but still thinking, "No God, that's okay. Not me. Let me just wait for somebody who speaks her language to come with me." Then I processed on to, "Okay, God, You're not letting this go. You're still bugging me about it, so I have to do something." I felt so nervous, but as soon as I started praying for her I felt confident that I was supposed to be praying for her. I was able to overcome my insecurity of stepping out and initiating prayer.

And so I did, all by myself. I didn't have anybody translating for me. I just was like, "Okay, God. I'm going to do this, and we'll see what You want to do here." So I started praying for her, and she was crying so hard. I had no idea what was wrong with her. I didn't know what she needed prayer for, so I laid my hands on her. I remember praying, "God, whatever You want to do here, just give her peace because she seems really shaken up and really nervous. Just give her peace."

As I was praying for her, she became relaxed, seemingly comforted by the Spirit. She sat down on the ground and eventually had laid down because she was crying so hard and uncontrollably. I remember that God said, "Lay your hand on her stomach and pray for her there." And I was like, "Her stomach? That's awkward. I don't really want to do that, and I don't think she would want me to touch her stomach either." I was still by myself and I didn't know what I was doing, but I just did it.

I remember praying that God would give her peace and that if she were in need of healing that she would be healed. Then her stomach became very warm, which was kind of intimidating to me. But I just kept praying for peace, but at the same time it was like God was saying, "Pray for her to be able to take a deep breath and let Me refresh her and she can breathe in My Spirit." So I started praying just that. I was praying out loud, but she didn't understand a word I said. But as soon as I said, "Lord, just let her breathe You in. Let her take a deep breath," she did, she took this huge deep breath. After that, she was completely peaceful. She stopped crying. Her eyes were closed and she was restful. She probably laid there five or ten more minutes as I just sat with her and prayed quietly.

Then one of the Mexicans from our team came over and wanted to talk to her a little bit and see if she knew the Lord. She said that she did know the Lord, but she was very scared because a week ago she had been diagnosed with cancer in her stomach. I was like, "Okay. I just prayed for her stomach. That's cool." Then he translated that she was nervous and that they said it was terminal, but she was grateful because she knew that the Lord had touched her that day. And I was like, "Yeah, okay." Like, "I've never witnessed a miracle and I really would love to, but it's little ole me and I don't speak your language, and I'm just a white American teenage girl with braces." I didn't really understand how the Holy Spirit worked at that point in my life. Just after that she stood up and left.

That was the end of the first week, and we were there for a whole other week after that. At this time, we had been traveling throughout the city to different sites. She apparently had been trying to follow us around and tried to talk to us. When she finally caught up to us in a different part of the city, you could tell the Lord touched her.

She shared with us that during the second week, she went back in for a treatment for her cancer and they did another scan and she was cancer-free—like completely healed! She was so excited to share that, and she said, "It's all because you prayed for me."

That's probably the biggest miracle that I've witnessed. It was one of the single most faith-building instances where my trust and my faith in Him, in what He could do, grew leaps and bounds. He was able to show me, "It doesn't matter what you do. If I want to do something and you let Me, I'll do it. As long as you're a willing vessel, I'll use you." But it was a confidence thing. I had to get past my fear, and then I had to trust God that He could work no matter what I did or didn't do.

Discussion Questions

1. Who are the people or types of people you have difficulty engaging in conversation? Why and what can you learn from recognizing these people patterns?
2. What topics do you have difficulty discussing with others? Why and what can you learn from recognizing these topical patterns?
3. What types of situational or environment patterns make it more or less likely that you will engage someone in conversation? Why are you impacted by certain situational factors and what can you learn from identifying these patterns?
4. Which thoughts and emotions from the list of conversational barriers have the biggest impact on you personally when it comes to engaging in divine opportunities?

Chapter 7
Turning Points

A *turning point* is defined as a moment when a person makes a decision to engage or ignore a conversational opportunity that changes the trajectory of a conversation, relationship, or even a life in subtle or significant ways.

The relational decisions that are made during these turning points can mean the difference between experiencing a divine opportunity or a missed opportunity. They can mean the difference between being obedient or disobedient to God's promptings, the difference between the thrill of conversational adventure or the regret of inaction, or the difference between a clear conscience or a conscience riddled with what-if doubts. I'm not trying to be a drama queen here (well, maybe a little bit), but you need to understand that these turning points may produce only subtle, perhaps trivial, changes in your life or others' lives, if any noticeable change at all. But they could also turn out to be a *really big deal*—totally life-altering and eternally impactful.

Turning points can occur anywhere along that spectrum of mattering a little (subtle, maybe trivial changes) to mattering a lot (life altering, eternally impactful). The trouble is that it's difficult to predict which turning points will lead to which outcomes. If you don't want to miss out on any of the gifts of opportunity God has for you, your safest bet is to be observant, optimistic, and obedient toward His conversational calling.

In life, we can count on enduring either one of two kinds of pain: we will "experience the pain of discipline or the pain of regret."[46] Read the following stories and think about this idea of turning points in everyday life. Consider the possible level of importance for what may have unfolded as a result of each interaction.

The following missed opportunity for a divine appointment comes from Jean, a fifty-nine-year-old marketing manager. This opportunity occurred years ago, when she was working in the insurance industry and driving home from work one evening.

> One day I was driving through a local neighborhood after finishing an inspection for work, when I pulled up to a stop sign. As I was stopped there, I looked over to my right and saw this really run-down house. I mean, it was just really beat up and things had been let go. It was in that moment that I felt God saying to me, "Jean, you need to go up to that house and ask the family what you can do for them."
>
> I then looked closer at the house, which I thought for sure was abandoned. Upon a second look, however, I could see toys all over the fenced-in yard. I thought to myself, "Oh my, people do live in this house—how awful." The house was just so run-down. And again, I felt God saying, "You need to go help them."
>
> I turned again to look at this house, and I just thought to myself, "What am I supposed to do? How am I going to walk up and say God just sent me here to help you?" I had no clue what I was going to do or say, and I was so embarrassed at the thought of that awkward moment and uncomfortable conversation. I didn't know how to just walk up to a strange house and say that God sent me and I'm not sure why. I really felt so dumb, embarrassed, and unsure of myself, unsure of the situation, and unsure of what would come from that interaction that I just couldn't bear to go through with it. So I just drove off.
>
> Well, two of days later I was at home watching the evening news and I saw a story about a local house that had burned to the ground. As soon as I heard the story, I immediately knew that it was the house God had led me toward just days earlier. I drove by the house the next day, and of course it was that exact house that had burned down.
>
> What had happened was that they had the gas turned off because the family couldn't pay the bills. And this was at the end of the year, when it was getting quite cold, so the family had to use

a space heater. Well, this family had a number of children with the youngest just being an infant. They had put the infant in his carrier and covered him with a blanket and put the space heater beside him. During the night the infant kicked his cover onto the space heater and it caught fire. Everyone in the family got out of the house except for the infant. The little baby had died in the house fire.

As soon as I heard that story I knew what I was supposed to do for that family. I was supposed to get the gas turned back on. I missed that opportunity.

I realize that this is certainly an extreme example. Divine opportunities are not always a matter of life or death. However, it's important for you to be mindful of the spectrum of possibilities. Obsessing or stressing out over your role isn't the answer, either, of course—you must maintain a healthy, life-giving, and motivational level of responsibility about the outcomes of those promptings that you choose to engage in or ignore, as well as those turning point decisions you make for better or worse. For it is God who gets the glory for the divine opportunities and it is God who redeems the missed opportunities. We should not punish ourselves for the negative consequences of inaction, nor should we ever exalt ourselves for the positive outcomes of our actions.

Hope Deferred Makes the Heart Sick

Jean's experience is not unlike many others who have engaged in divine opportunities and missed opportunities. Her conversation was sidetracked, and her turning point decision was negatively influenced by her conversational barriers, as discussed in chapter 6. As you revisit Jean's story, you will notice that she mentions her particular conversational barriers—her fear of embarrassment, her concern for uncertainty, and her hesitancy because of the potential awkwardness of the situation. In the end, it was these relational fears that she let influence her decision negatively, and ultimately they kept her from obeying God's prompting.

We shouldn't allow fear and other negative emotions act as barriers to conversation. Instead, we should view those negative emotions as markers indicating that we are on to something with promise and potential. Everyone experiences similar fears, worries, and concerns *following* their initial promptings and *prior* to their turning point decisions. Regardless of whether you are an auto mechanic, professor, police officer, nurse, or pastor, you will hit a point in the process where you are forced to *secede* or *succeed* through and in light of those emotional barriers.

The three most common barriers to potential divine opportunity conversations include fearing embarrassment, fearing rejection, and doubting whether or not the prompting is actually coming from God. Those who succumb to the fear of embarrassment are, in effect, turning the moment over to their fleeting emotions rather than turning the moment over to God and trusting that "whom He calls, He also equips."[47] People who get sidetracked by the fear of rejection ultimately choose to do the rejecting rather than be rejected. In this sense, these people would rather reject God's prompting than to risk being rejected by another person in conversation.

Finally, those who find themselves debating whether or not the prompting is truly coming from God often fail to ask themselves, "Regardless of the exact origin, what's the *worst* thing that could happen if I act on this conversational prompting?" Based upon the interviews that I have conducted, there is far greater risk in ignoring these conversational opportunities than there is in engaging in them.

This turning point conundrum, engage or ignore, takes me to Proverbs 13:12: "Hope deferred makes the heart sick, but a longing fulfilled is a tree of life." Several of the Christians with whom I have spoken over the years have been able to recount missed opportunities from as far back as twenty years in the past. Even in the retelling of a missed opportunity from two decades earlier, these individuals' eyes would still well up with tears, and their voices shook with emotion. Their hearts feel sick over a hope deferred, because they let down an opportunity in fear rather than rising to the challenge in faithfulness.

In contrast, others with whom I spoke have responded to divine promptings and experienced spiritual growth as a result, even in situations when the conversation itself didn't seem to result in any identifiable outcome. The reason these responsive people still grew in their relationship with God was not through a life-altering conversation, but as part of a simple act of obedience—they acted on the desire that God gave them and that was enough.

There is yet another way to frame our relational fears, worries, or concerns during these turning point moments as well. In fact, those who experience divine opportunities have been able to use their fears in life-giving ways. They realize that those fears signal one of two things. First, those fears can indicate spiritual warfare. The enemy attempts to keep us from what God is trying to accomplish through us for the greater good of ourselves and others.

Second, those fears could be a sign that we do need to proceed with some caution. Divine opportunities, at times, can be difficult conversations—"difficult" in the sense that they may be riddled with emotions for both parties. These conversations may be addressing a touchy topic, and the outcome and ramifications of the conversation could be extremely uncertain. Therefore, those fears we may experience beforehand can be a wonderful signal to slow down, to be thoughtful with the approach, and to be sensitive in choosing words. When we heed these signals and proceed with both courage and heightened awareness, we are able to draw people in, to help them feel safe, and to accept the conversational opportunity as a gift from God. When we recognize those conversational barriers and negative emotions as flags marking a situation with promise and potential, then we can begin to use them in positive and productive ways.

Consider Jean's missed opportunity in contrast with the following divine opportunity from my father-in-law. David's divine opportunity has its own elements of uncertainty, distraction, and comfort-zone stretching. However, he was able to overcome those barriers and to make an obedient turning point decision.

> A couple of years ago I got in a car accident, and the back of my van was smashed. At the time, I didn't have a regular auto body place where I could take my vehicle, but I happened to learn about a local place through a mailer. As I checked it out, they seemed to do good work at a reasonable price. So I left my van with Sergei, the owner, for the work to be done. Sergei called me up when the back end had been fixed, and I later dropped by to pick it up.
>
> On the day of pick-up, I had my wife drop me off at the auto body shop. She then headed back home while I was doing a quick inspection, making the payment, and wrapping things up. As I got around to writing the check to Sergei, I felt like God was laying it on my heart to pray for him. Keep in mind this wasn't the most spiritual of atmospheres. There was hard rock music blaring from the speakers in the shop, and the overall environment was very rough. Needless to say, it wasn't a place of comfort for me. I didn't exactly feel at home in that auto garage, and I hadn't experienced an immediate connection with Sergei to begin with. In fact, those distractions caused me a brief moment of hesitation. But despite feeling uncomfortable and out of place, I could not ignore this prompting for prayer that God was laying on me. I knew that God wanted me to pray for this man.

So I asked him, "Sergei, is there anything that I can pray with you about?" Sergei quickly replied, "Oh, I'm not a man of faith, I don't think there is anything you can pray for me about." At the time, I really felt like there was something God had positioned me to pray with him about but I didn't want to press the issue. I let it go. I finished up paying for the van and headed outside.

Just as I opened the door and was about to climb inside, Sergei ran up to me. He said, "You know what? There *is* something that you can pray for my wife about. We have been trying, unsuccessfully, to have a baby for about five years. This has been a growing frustration for my wife and I; she has been crying about this for the past month. And just this morning she had a doctor's appointment, and the doctor gave her a final checkup and told her that she would never be able to have a baby. This final diagnosis from the doctor put her over the edge. She came home crying, and she was still crying when I left to come to work. Can you pray for her?"

I said, "I would be happy to, Sergei. Sergei, can I tell you that I believe in divine opportunities, and I believe that God put me here today because He knows what you are going through, and He cares about the intimate details of your life." And then I prayed. I prayed that God would be with his wife during this difficult time of her life. And as I prayed that (I felt like God was paving the way for something greater) God would give them the desires of their heart, and that God would give his wife the ability to have a baby.

As I finished praying, I don't know exactly what came over me, but I said, "Sergei, I want you to call me and tell me when your son is born." I reached into my wallet and I pulled out a business card and handed it to him. Then we said our goodbyes, and I headed off in my van.

Well, about a year later, I was in my office on campus working when I received a phone call. As I answered, the man on the other line said, "Is this David Watson?" I said, "Yes." He said, "Did you have a van that got the back end repaired about a year ago at SBB Auto Body?" I said, "Yes." He said, "This is Sergei. You prayed with me the day that you picked up your van, about a year ago, for my wife and I to have a baby?" I said, "Yes, Sergei, that was me." He said, "Well, I wanted to call you and let you know that my baby boy was born. And I wanted to thank you for praying for my wife and I that day. And I wanted you to know that we have decided to name our boy David!"

When I went home that day, I told my wife about the whole experience, the initial prayer, and the phone call about Sergei's baby boy. My wife was so excited that she wanted to pick up a gift, drop it by the auto body shop, and meet Sergei. So later that week we did just that. As we pulled up and walked into the auto body shop, it immediately struck me how different the place looked. Where there used to be worn partitions and tattered posters, there was fresh paint and clean walls. And those speakers that used to be blaring rock music were now playing Christian music.

As we approached Sergei, he had a huge smile on his face. He took us in and began showing us picture after picture after picture. He had to have had 250 pictures of his son that he quickly flipped through. And then Sergei told us that he and his wife had turned such a wonderful corner in their lives, and that they were attending a local church and growing in their faith.

One thing that always strikes me about David's divine opportunities is that he never seems to require much convincing to follow through with the relational promptings that God puts in his heart. I wish I could say the same for myself. Even when David is put in less than ideal situations and could easily let himself get swept away with external distractions like an intense physical atmosphere, lewd pictures, and disruptive music, he still keeps himself on track to triumph in the turning point decisions he needs to make.

However, when it comes to being able to survive and thrive in the face of all our fears, worries, concerns, and hesitations, I think it is fair to say that David would be in the minority and I would fall in the majority—i.e., those who end up succumbing to negative emotions more often than not.

I have spent a great deal of time thinking about what might help myself and others achieve a state of mind, spirituality, and faithfulness that would enable us to forge ahead with optimistic obedience, like David—even when we might be overly busy, when the atmosphere might be less than inviting, or when we are feeling shy and timid. The following is a practical method for helping us all pursue the desires of our heart, call upon the Holy Spirit, tap into our emotions, and become "turning-point gurus."

Pause Button Therapy

There is a relational skill that can help us all survive the temptations, fears, worries, concerns, and hesitations wrapped up in our turning points.

This skill is something that psychology experts Martin and Marion Shirran have called "Pause Button Therapy" (PBT).[48]

This form of therapy can have incredible effects on our ability to make the best possible choice in these turning point moments of our lives. PBT instructs people to approach any decision with the mindset that they hold a mental "remote control" to their own life. This gives people the power to "hit the pause button" on their life prior to making any decision, whether big or small. The pause (or "decision delay") can be for any length of time—a few seconds, one minute, ten minutes, an hour, one day, or even one week. It simply gives people the needed time and mental space to process through their options in a way that leads to the best possible choice while giving them the mental and emotional motivation to do so.

The trick is that PBT also coaches people to utilize the full range of any remote control—pause, rewind, fast-forward, and play.[49] The rewind function in this case allows people to revisit their past—past relationships, decisions, emotions, and experiences. The fast-forward function allows people to look to the future and thoughtfully consider what outcome they foresee, based upon making one decision over another. Finally, once people are able to revisit their past and fast-forward to the corresponding potential future, they can then come back to the moment in the present and make the best possible decision. They simply press "play" and live out that thoughtful choice. The PBT motto is stop, think, decide, act.[50] PBT allows people to *respond* rather than *react* to various triggers, temptations, or barriers in their everyday life.

If we go back and review Jean's missed opportunity outside the run-down house, we can see how she may have benefited from PBT. Unfortunately, Jean is one of those people (like myself) who need a little more motivation than David needs in order to be obedient to God's prompting. This is especially the case when the prompting is leading us to stretch our comfort zone and requiring us to overcome one or more relational barriers. Most people do not have a game plan for overcoming such tensions between the difficulty of being obedient *versus* the ease of being disobedient in the turning point moments of divine opportunities.

How might the outcome of Jean's opportunity have changed if she had been equipped to motivate herself and to work her way through those barriers? Perhaps before she drove off she could have thought back to a past missed opportunity—rewind—and contemplated the details of a previous act of disobedience. She could have allowed herself to consider *quickly* and *deeply* the implications for herself, her relationship with God, and her impact or lack thereof on another person. This moment of rewind includes the brief reliving of the feelings of regret, conviction, or guilt she may have felt in the past.

Jean could have envisioned the future state that she would most desire for herself and her walk with Christ—fast-forward. She could imagine desires fulfilled or hopes deferred in the future, as impacted by each act of obedience and disobedience. "Hope deferred makes the heart sick, but a longing fulfilled is a tree of life" (Proverbs 13:12). Then she could have come back to the moment in the car and been motivated to choose the potentially awkward yet eternally rewarding path—play—by honoring God's prompting that day.

Tapping into the Power of PBT

There are a few elements crucial to using PBT correctly. The first is to practice using the mental pause button.[51] Much like any skill, it is vitally important that you overlearn this technique. In order for you to rely upon PBT in a hurried and emotion-laden moment, you must have incorporated PBT as your default way of handling decisions. This only comes from repetition and practice. Otherwise, you will continue to make decisions in keeping with your same old habits. Dr. Anthony Muhammad has said, "Dispositions eat knowledge and skill for breakfast." I could teach you all sorts of communication skills like PBT, but if you don't practice them to the point of rewiring your dispositional tendencies, then you will fail to utilize those skills when they are needed most. Communication skills are like muscles; they need to be exercised often so they can be called upon during relational game-time decisions.

Second, when you rewind and revisit your past experiences, relationships, and choices, you must be willing to relive the negative emotions that resulted from poor choices, or the positive emotions that resulted from good choices.[52] Strive to *feel* the emotions from the past. It is the emotional experience and emotional appeal that will motivate you to avoid past mistakes and to repeat positive behaviors. Our past mistakes are why we experience feelings of guilt, regret, and conviction to begin with. God hardwired us to experience those emotions so that we will be motivated to make life-giving relational decisions in the future. If you don't tap into that emotion from the past, your rewind attempt will not fulfill its purpose.

Third, when you fast-forward to consider your desired positive outcome, or the possible negative outcome from alternative choices, it is important that you use your imagination to fill in as much detail as possible.[53] Truly consider the emotional state for yourself and the other person that may be impacted by your present choice. Envision what your life, relationship, and spiritual connection could be like if you choose one path over another. Details matter.

When fast-forwarding, the details of the possible positive and negative effects will fuel your ambition and motivation for the present. As you imagine this fast-forward sequence, keep in mind that each small act of obedience builds your connection and relationship with God. Regardless of whether it leads to noticeable change in the conversation or relationship between you and the other person, that small act of obedience leads to an improved ability to recognize and respond to God's presence in your life. And that should be a desirable future for us all.

Fourth, PBT experts have found it helpful for people to visualize themselves standing at a fork in the road, the turning point, and envision the paths to the right and left.[54] Even label them "the good road" and "the bad road" based upon your alternative options. This helps people feel empowered by the choices they have and the personal decision that awaits. At your imaginary fork in the road, ask yourself, "Where does the path of obedience and the path of disobedience lead me in the short- and long-term view of my life?" Does one lead to a clear conscience, or to a conscience riddled with regret? From there, simply do your best, and let God take care of the rest.

Finally, before hitting the play button and making your final decision of action or inaction, there is one last technique that I encourage you to try out. I challenge you to look someone in the eyes. Instead of allowing yourself to see a mere man or woman, imagine you are looking at the face of Jesus. Imagine how you would respond if Jesus were the person toward whom you were being prompted, and consider the passage from Matthew 25:35–40:

> For I was hungry and you gave me something to eat, I was thirsty and you gave me something to drink, I was a stranger and you invited me in, I needed clothes and you clothed me, I was sick and you looked after me, I was in prison and you came to visit me.
>
> Then the righteous will answer him, "Lord, when did we see you hungry and feed you, or thirsty and give you something to drink? When did we see you a stranger and invite you in, or needing clothes and clothe you?"

> The King will reply, "I tell you the truth, whatever you did for one of the least of these brothers of mine, you did for me."

This is one of the most powerful and emotional techniques you will ever need to overcome your fears, worries, or concerns in order to follow your divine promptings and engage in conversation. Once you have basked in the reflected glory of Jesus in the very person before you, you may say a quick prayer, "God, may You give me both the boldness and sensitivity needed for this moment. May Your Holy Spirit direct my thoughts and words. In Jesus Christ's name, amen."

⏸ PAUSE—REWIND—FAST-FORWARD—JESUS—PRAY—PLAY

Practicing and Mastering PBT

PBT is one of the easiest and most effective techniques for helping you overcome your conversational barriers and make the best decision possible as you stumble upon these turning points. You can begin to practice this technique in one of three ways.

First, you can set up imaginary divine opportunity scenarios for yourself. Walk through a scenario in your mind, being realistic about how you would like to *respond* as opposed to how you would most likely *react*. It's a lot like the imagined interaction version of that TV show *What Would You Do?* You can begin this exercise by reviewing the various divine opportunities that have been shared in this book and thoughtfully considering what you would have done in each case. The key is to be as honest and realistic as possible with what you yourself would have most likely done in that specific situation. You don't do yourself any favors by giving yourself more credit than you realistically deserve. Be brutally candid with yourself about your level of mindfulness in recognizing God's promptings, your level of obedience to God's conversational calling, and your level of sensitivity to read the emotional cues of others.

Second, you can think about your own missed opportunities from your past and relive them in your mind utilizing PBT to think about what you could have done differently if you had taken the time to pause, rewind, fast-forward, see Jesus, pray, and then press play. This would be a twist on the TV show approach above, which could, for our purposes, be called *What Would You Do Differently?* Don't beat yourself up over these past missed opportunities, but instead take advantage of them to learn from your mistakes and to strategize about what you would like to do if you ever were to face a similar situation in the future. PBT experts suggest trying to plan out your response to life decisions in advance by completing the following statement for various situations, "If _____ occurs, I will do _____."[55]

Third, you can begin to practice this technique for everyday decisions. Rather than trying to utilize PBT for the first time during hurried and stressful interactions, try putting PBT into practice for interactions or decisions of less importance where your level of stress is low and your level of creativity is high. The PBT approach will come more naturally and will be easier to execute more effectively in stressful moments *after* you have mastered it during the mundane moments of everyday life. After all, "kneejerk reactions are not chosen in the moment." Our reactions come from our cumulative experiences, thoughts, and past decisions.[56] So we must work to break down our self-sabotaging thoughts, build up our self-confidence, and find peace in the grace, mercy, and motivation of Jesus.

Repurposing the Pain of Past Missed Opportunities

Finally, here is what I love most of all about this PBT approach. By rewinding into our past and experiencing the negative emotions that accompanied our previous missed opportunities, we acknowledge that God can repurpose our past mistakes, our past heartaches, and our past regrets of inaction—and we feel motivated to ask Him to do so. During moments of rewind, we permit those past missed opportunity emotions to fuel our current motivation in present and future divine opportunities. In doing so, those past experiences are redeemed, fulfilled, and brought to the foot of the cross, as if to say—what the devil meant for harm, God has used for good, the saving and redeeming of His people (Genesis 50:20).

I love this because God never stops trying to use us to fulfill His many purposes for all His sons and daughters here on earth. No matter how many times we miss His divine promptings, no matter how many times we are disobedient, no matter how many times we fall victim to our fears, worries, or concerns, God is continuing His good work in us and through us for our own sanctification and for the betterment of others.

If we use PBT as a form of "spiritual time-travel," we can rewind and go back to our past missed opportunities and we can convert the pain of regret into a tool to help us overcome our self-sabotaging thoughts in the present. As tough as it may be for people like Vicky who have missed opportunities, perhaps God makes us aware of harsh outcomes so that we would have the motivation needed to overcome and redeem such experiences in the future. No missed opportunity is wasted by God. He redeems them all in His own unique way. And I love Him for it. Let your faith in God, and your faith in His prompting, lead you through the turning points of your conversations.

Discussion Questions

1. Each of you share a missed opportunity that you have had in the past.
2. Put yourself in your discussion partners' place. What would you have most likely done if you were in a similar situation?
3. How might you approach barriers differently if you were to face similar turning points in the future?
4. How does your faith in God influence your willingness to be obedient and to embrace even the most awkward and uncomfortable of conversations?
5. How have you seen God repurpose the pain from your past missed opportunities?

Tasks

1. Revisit Jean's story at the beginning of this chapter and be brutally honest with yourself: if you were to find yourself in Jean's shoes that day, being prompted by God to approach some random run-down house to ask strangers what you might do for them, what would you have done? How would you have handled that turning point? Would you have been obedient, or would you have also driven off?
2. Think of a divine opportunity or missed opportunity scenario from your own life and carefully consider how you could use PBT to drive your conversational actions and change the outcome of that interaction.

Chapter 8

Optimistic Obedience

The only thing that counts is faith expressing itself through love.

—Galatians 5:6

Optimistic: to expect the most favorable outcome.[57]

Obedience: submissive compliance.[58]

A Divine Opportunity

This first person who comes to my mind when I think about someone who regularly embraces optimistic obedience toward God's promptings is my father-in-law, David. When he experiences a prompting to have a conversation with someone or pray for someone, it's as good as done. He may occasionally have a slight hesitancy or even experience the same initial feelings of awkwardness or concern that others have, but it doesn't take him long to turn his focus from those feelings back to God. From there it's just a matter of letting the Spirit lead him into the unknown, and doing so with an optimistic attitude that God will come through.

David likes to picture himself as the spiritual Indiana Jones, always up for an adventure, exploration, and discovery. Below is another divine opportunity of his, which I will use to illustrate some of the key factors involved for developing this sense of optimistic obedience in all of us.

Many years ago I was preaching at a youth camp in Harrisburg, Pennsylvania, there were about 2,500 young adults in all. It was a huge gathering of Christian youth. As I was preaching, about midway through my message, my eyes fell on a young lady about halfway back. When I saw her I could sense that God was putting something on my heart.

This wasn't in my notes, it wasn't planned, and it wasn't thought-out, but I knew that God wanted to intervene in her life. It's always an amazing thing, here are all these young adults but God is particularly concerned about one young woman who is sitting in the middle of all of them. He put this thought in my mind, "I want you to give her worth, value, and dignity."

Now I'm going to be honest: this was a little awkward. But you know, God doesn't ask you if you're ready. God doesn't get permission when He wants to do something. He doesn't ask if you are comfortable with the situation. Instead, He asks, "Are you available?" He doesn't ask if you are prepared or if you have the credentials. It's just, "Are you available for Me to flow through you to do something holy?" That will be, by the way, unexplainable. We are not able to understand it. The only one who will understand it will be God.

At this point in my sermon, I was thinking, "How in the world can I do this?" And I remembered when I was at Central Bible College a man came through with a beautiful illustration, one that I found touching and one that proved to be useful here too. And I just said, "Folks, I feel like I have to take a break in the middle of my sermon. I feel like this is one of those holy moments that I must be obedient to God."

I took out a twenty-dollar bill, and as I was walking down toward this young woman I said, "Here is a nice twenty-dollar bill. How many of you would like this twenty-dollar bill?" And of course everyone's hands shot up. "Well, how about if I crumble it all up, now how many of you would still want it?" All their hands still shot up. "How about if I throw it down on the ground and rubbed into the carpet with my shoe, now how many of you would still want it?" All their hands again shot up.

I then went over to the young woman sitting in the middle of the pew (and I had to crawl over about three people by the way in order to get to her). They all thought, "What is he doing?" And honestly, I didn't know what I was doing either. Holy moments are the moments that are pure God. Revelation is where God does something that is beyond you.

I said to this young lady, "I just want you to understand that I've done all of this to this twenty-dollar bill—I have wrinkled it, I have thrown it down, I have put my shoe on it and it's now dirty—would you still take it?" And without hesitation she grabbed it out of my hand and she said, "I sure will take it." I said, "Why are you taking this twenty-dollar bill? It's all dirty, crumpled, and worn." And she said, "I can still spend it."

And I said, "That's the truth that I want you to see. There's value and worth and dignity, and no matter what people do, no matter how people see you, it's the value that God sees in you. And people may not always understand you. In fact, people may make fun of you, people may say mean things about you, hurtful things, terrible things, but God wants you to know that He has a value in you that people don't give you. You have a worth that people don't give you. You have dignity that people don't give you, and no matter what your past has been He's got a future for you."

I did what God told me to do. I wrote on the twenty-dollar bill value, worth, and dignity. I gave it to her and said, "God wants you to have this and for you to look at it every day. For some reason out of this great big group of people, God has this message for you." That was all. I then went back and finished my message as planned, closed out the event, and headed back home.

Fast-forward many many years later. I was preaching at a pastor's seminar in Indiana, Pennsylvania, and during one of the breaks I was standing in the lobby and a dignified woman came up to me and said, "Sir, you don't know who I am. And it's been a long time since we met. But I read in the paper that you were going to be speaking in Indiana, so I drove up from Pittsburgh."

She said, "A number of years ago, when I was a teenager, sixteen years of age, you had no way of knowing, but my mom and dad were in the middle of a terrible, ugly divorce. You had no way of knowing, but my whole world was torn apart. At that time I went to a youth convention with a friend of mine. I had no real relationship with God. I had religion, but I never knew about a personal relationship with God—that He could care about me personally."

Then she said, "In that youth revival you came to me." Then she reached in her purse and pulled out the twenty-dollar bill that I had given to her. And I looked at my handwriting and there it was—worth, value, dignity. And she said, "I put that on my mirror and every time I got up I looked at it, and it was like God spoke to me. I can do anything because my worth and value doesn't come from what others may say or think, my God gives me worth, value, and dignity." She continued, "All these years later, I'm now the head of the pediatric department in one of the biggest hospitals in Pittsburgh, Pennsylvania."

God knew that this girl, in the huge crowd of young people, needed a love note from Him personally to get her through the tough times and to remind her that He believes she was valued. It didn't matter what had happened in her past; that was a holy moment for her. God helped her understand that He had something special in store for her. Even though people wanted to hold her back, God had a plan for her. He set her apart, and instilled worth, value, and dignity.

What an incredible story. There are many different lessons we could extract from this story. The two that I would like to focus on are the inconvenience of the prompting and David's optimistic obedience to the prompting. First of all, this prompting that David experienced wasn't exactly convenient for him. In fact, he could have experienced the prompting in the middle of his sermon and had an attitude of situational perfectionism. David could have thought, "This isn't great timing. I'm in the middle of a message I prepared for a couple thousand people, and you want me to disrupt it for this one person? How about I keep an eye out for her after I finish my message and I'll talk with her on the side and explore this later?" There are all sorts of ways he could have turned away and rationalized his disobedience to the prompting and continued on with his message, never knowing what he had passed up.

As David stated, "God doesn't ask you if you're ready. God doesn't get permission when He wants to do something. He doesn't ask if you are comfortable with the situation. Instead, He asks, 'Are you available?' He doesn't ask if you are prepared or if you have the credentials. It's just, 'Are you available for Me to flow through you to do something holy?'" I pray that we all are increasing in our faith so that we are prepared to accept God's calling for a conversation, an interaction, or a prayer with the person He is putting in our path. If we turn away from His prompting, we may be robbing someone of a life-changing experience. In fact, we may be robbing ourselves of a faith-building experience as well. Not only was this young woman's life transformed by that divine opportunity, but David's faith in God and his spiritual self-confidence were greatly transformed as well.

Turning Toward in Obedience

The second part of David's story that I want to focus on is his optimistic obedience, and how we can take up a similar mentality ourselves. To do so, I want to come back to some work by relationship expert Dr. John Gottman. I know what you must be thinking at this point, "Shouldn't this dude be citing the apostle Paul, or maybe Matthew, Mark, Luke, or John, rather than John Gottman?" I probably should, but I'm trying to be optimistically obedient to the message God has put in my heart for this book, which is a practical playbook for approaching divine opportunities. The best way I know how to approach that is through my academic man-crush, John Gottman.

When it comes to relationships, Dr. Gottman continually stresses how important it is for partners to turn toward one another's emotional bids for attention. I believe it is equally important for us to turn toward God's bids for our attention as well, and there are some practical spiritual takeaways for us here. Gottman discovered four different ways that couples respond to one another's emotional bids in conversation. These include (1) turning away, (2) turning against, (3) turning toward, and (4) turning toward enthusiastically. These four types of turns are equally as important when it comes to thinking about how you respond to God's spiritual and situational bids for your attention. I want to focus on turning toward and enthusiastically turning toward as examples of how we can express an optimistic obedience to our promptings from God.

Turning Toward

Turning toward an emotional bid requires first recognizing the bid and then responding to the bid by communicating acknowledgement and acceptance. One example Dr. Gottman gives is of a couple who is sitting in the living room of an apartment. The husband is on the couch reading an article on his cell phone, while the wife is looking out the window as boats pass by along the water. The wife turns to the husband and says, "Wow, look at that boat. What a beautiful boat." What seems like a casual passing comment is actually an invitation being extended to the husband to join her in conversation or even to join her at the window. Rather than ignoring his wife's bid (which is turning away) or getting annoyed by her interruption (which is turning against) the husband turns toward her emotional bid. He looks up from his cell phone, leans forward, peeks out the window, and says, "Yeah, that is a nice boat." This guy may not win husband of the year, but he has at least turned toward his wife's emotional bid in some way.

In our application of obedience to God's promptings, this is the first of two levels of obedience. In David's example, he may have recognized God putting the thought in his head, "I want you to give her worth, value, and dignity." David could have turned toward God's bid in a number of ways. He could have tried to accommodate for the bid by trying to weave that thought into the message he was already working through, or he could have briefly paused in his message and then made some general remarks more focused on this thought, without fully engaging the young girl one-on-one. From this perspective, David would have at least been obediently turning toward God's prompting. This turn toward may have made an impact or perhaps may have left more to be desired from the moment. The writer of Proverbs wrote, "Do not withhold good from those who deserve it, when it is in your power to act" (Proverbs 3:27).

Sometimes this simple act of turning toward, even slightly, is a great first step to buy you more time as you continue to seek out what God is trying to tell you or what God is trying to guide you into. As we turn toward God's bids, we are opening ourselves up and inviting others to join us in conversation. In doing so, more about the person or situation may be revealed, which ultimately lets us in on where God is taking us. Below is one quick mindset check and two simple strategies for taking the initial steps of obedience for turning toward God's bids.

Mindset check. It's important not to put too much pressure on yourself. Remember to "do your best, and let God take care of the rest." I love that line—it's such a simple reminder that all God asks of us is obedience and faith expressing itself through love. God doesn't expect us to be in charge of outcomes and results. That's all in His hands. We plant the seed and God gives the increase. Take some pressure off of yourself. Not every conversation needs to be thought of as a life-altering moment. Perhaps paying someone attention in simple, good old-fashioned conversation is enough.

Strategy 1: Just walk across the room. Pastor Bill Hybels of Willow Creek Church wrote a great book entitled *Just Walk Across the Room.*[59] The title alone speaks volumes about what our first simple strategy should be for turning toward God's bids and moving toward conversation with others. This is a wonderful mind trick to help us avoid overthinking God's promptings and the ensuing conversation. You don't need to allow your mind to jump ahead to anxiety-producing thoughts about the details of the conversation or potential outcomes. Simply walk across the room, put your hand out, and introduce yourself. From there, let God direct your thoughts, words, and conversation.

This downsizing of divine opportunities to the first simple obedient act of walking across the room reminds me of a workout strategy known as the "One-Song Workout."[60] The one-song workout is a mental life-hack used to address the issue of well-intentioned people failing to get their workout in at the gym or at home. Far too many people have the desire to regularly exercise, but they continually fail to work out and live up to their fitness goals.

People start or end their day a little too tired or exhausted to get themselves motivated for a one- or two-hour workout before or after work. So not only do they fail to get their exercise, but they also take a hit to their self-esteem and self-worth because they couldn't live up to their goals. Does this sound familiar at all in comparison to our shortcomings with divine opportunities?

What researchers have done to address this fitness problem is to ask people to lower their expectations for their workout and workout time. Instead of setting the goal of a one- to two-hour workout, they redrafted their goal to simply workout for the length of one song; thus, the name one-song workout. Then the researchers told people that if they work out for the length of one song, they could stop working out at the end of the song with a clear conscience. Thus, they would have achieved their goal.

Granted, these people aren't going to end up in a Reebok cross-fit commercial as a result of working out for three minutes a day, but there was a surprising result. Not only did these people keep to the one-song workout far more often than those with greater, more impressive workout goals, but these people typically put in a full workout far beyond the length of the one song. What the researchers found was that the hardest part for people was simply starting the workout. Once they had started the workout—motivated by shrinking the goal to the length of one song—it was dramatically easier to continue for the remaining hour. The added bonus was that these people also raised their self-esteem in the process because they were achieving their goals and living up to their personal expectations far more often.

I have found the same to be true for conversation. Typically, the hardest part for people is starting a conversation. Once they start the conversation, however, it tends to flow naturally from there. Just walking across the room is the relational equivalent of the one-song workout. If you use this mental life-hack—staying focused on simply walking across the room to strike up friendly conversation—you will find yourself more relaxed and motivated to turn toward God's promptings. You will also likely encounter more regular spiritual and relational success, motivation, and increased self-confidence. Ultimately, this will lead you to small wins with a clear conscience and surprising results.

Strategy 2: Develop back-pocket questions. Having a few back-pocket questions that you can rely on after walking across the room will significantly improve your transition into conversation. I have found that some of the smoothest conversationalist's have strong, open-ended back-pocket questions that they can go to during lulls in conversation. Back-pocket questions are those that are prepared ahead of time that you can go to when you are looking to start conversation or when conversation seems to run dry. The idea is to think about questions ahead of time that you can ask that get people thinking and talking openly and freely. Back-pocket questions can explore any number of topics, although I would avoid anything that might lead to controversial or sensitive issues. Don't be that person. The most important factor is that these questions are open-ended.

Here's the basic difference between closed-ended and open-ended questions. Close-ended questions result in yes or no answers that leave both parties scrambling for the next line in the conversation. We've all been in those conversations where all that comes to mind are yes/no questions where the other person gives us one or two word answers and things get awkward. You're just thinking, "For the love, please throw me a bone and at least give me a bit of a response I can work with here." Close-ended questions also include those overstated questions like, "How are you doing?" Can we all just agree that no one actually cares how you are doing when they ask this question? If you responded with, "Not good at all, my dog just died," that person would be so caught off guard they wouldn't know what to do with themselves.

Open-ended questions, on the other hand, usually involve words like "why," "what," "describe," which all result in longer responses and keep people talking and conversation flowing. For example: What is one new thing happening for you? What is one thing you're excited about coming up? What is one thing that is going well for you right now? What is one thing that you're worried or concerned about right now? What is one thing that I can pray with you about? What does that tattoo mean to you? I've got some free time coming up to read a book; do you have a favorite book that you would recommend reading? What's your favorite app on your phone right now?

These back-pocket questions can include anything that starts or turns the conversation in a direction that gets people thinking and talking. The more you can get the other person reflecting about their own life and talking about themselves the better. The key is to take a genuine interest in the other person and exploring their response. Dale Carnegie, author of *How to Win Friends and Influence People*, once said, "You can make more friends in two months by becoming genuinely interested in people than you can in two years by trying to get others interested in you."[61] Do not underestimate what these back-pocket questions could lead you to in conversation. Test out a couple of your own back-pocket questions in a few upcoming conversational opportunities; you will be pleasantly surprised by the results.

Everyone has a life story to tell. These back-pocket questions are simply a gateway for opening up relational space for those stories to be shared, expressed, and heard. There is a great line in the movie *The Legend of Bagger Vance* with Will Smith. He says, "Ain't a soul on this entire earth that ain't got a burden to carry that they don't understand." Often divine opportunities are simply opportunities to explore other's stories, their unheard or untold stories. Our job is to create space in our everyday lives to be observant and responsive to opportunities to hear about the burdens that others may be carrying around. This is true for friends and foes, as American poet and Harvard professor Henry Longfellow once said, "If we could read the secret history of our enemies, we should find in each man's life sorrow and suffering enough to disarm all hostility." Please take time to look for opportunities to explore others' personal histories in conversation, even if it is through the slightest effort of turning toward others.

Enthusiastically Turning Toward

This is where it gets fun. Enthusiastically turning toward an emotional bid is a turn toward that has excitement, interest, curiosity, responsive compassion, or attentive empathy. In the Gottman example, the husband is again on the couch reading the article on the cell phone, and the wife says, "Wow, look at that boat. What a beautiful boat." This time the husband puts down his cell phone, walks over to the window, peeks out the window, and says, "Yeah, that is a beautiful boat. Have you ever thought about us renting a boat for a weekend and just heading out on the water with just the two of us? Wouldn't that be fun!" This husband has just hit a home run with his enthusiastic turn toward his wife's casual emotional bid. It's likely that the wife will reciprocate the play in conversation and what seemed to be a low-key comment has now turned into a fun, playful conversation.

Enthusiastically turning toward is the second level of obedience to God's bids for our attention. When David recognized God putting the thought in his head—"I want you to give her worth, value, and dignity"—he enthusiastically turned toward God's bid. He recognized the prompting, thought about it for a moment, recalled the twenty-dollar bill illustration, and then decided to jump into optimistic obedience with both feet. He straight cannonballed into a pool of obedience. He didn't dip a toe in, he didn't ask what the temperature of the water was like, he didn't jog around to work up a sweat; instead, he launched himself in wholeheartedly. That is what optimistic obedience is all about—a wholehearted, enthusiastic turn toward God by turning toward others. I would be willing to bet that out of 2,500 youth present that day at the convention there were several others, beside the one young woman, who were just as moved by the ripple that was created by David's cannonball of obedience.

This type of optimistic obedience reminds me of the improvisational comedy rule "Yes, and…" In improv comedy training, all comedians are taught roughly the same set of rules for participating in a comedic scene. The most common rule is that of the "Yes, and…" This implies that each person should accept what the other brings into the scene, and then add to the suggestion or comment. If one actor says, "How did we get on this lifeboat?" it's important for the other actor to avoid turning away or against this suggestion. It would kill the momentum of the scene and morale of the other actor if the person responded, "Lifeboat? No, we are actually in a wheelbarrow." Successful improv comedies would instead enthusiastically turn toward the comment by accepting and adding to the original lifeboat suggestion, "The pirates finally got sick of hearing you sing 'Hakuna Matata' and they threw us overboard."

"Yes, and…" is the response from Triple O Christians when they recognize a divine opportunity. They turn toward God's original bid, accept the prompting, and seek out creative ways to move in the direction God is leading them. David said yes to God's prompting, "I want you to give her worth, value, and dignity." Then he added to that original prompting by creatively integrating the twenty-dollar bill illustration. What resulted was a powerfully fun and inspiring spiritual scene. In what ways could you approach God's divine promptings as if you are an improv actor in a scene that God has just initiated with an opening suggestion? How can you play-fully and creatively say "Yes, and..." to God with an attitude of enthusiasm and optimism?

People who enthusiastically and optimistically turn toward God's promptings and bids do so with the knowledge and assurance that their labor in the Lord is not in vain. Paul wrote to the Corinthians: "There-fore, my dear brothers, stand firm. Let nothing move you. Always give yourselves fully to the work of the Lord, because you know that your labor in the Lord is not in vain" (1 Corinthians 15:58). There may not always be immediate results, but through an eternal perspective we can engage divine opportunities knowing that there may be ripples in eternity that we may not ever recognize this side of heaven. These divine opportunities are con-versations that last *in* eternity. After all, even in David's divine opportunity he had to wait some twenty years to find out how his optimistic obedience played out in that moment with that young woman.

Our enthusiastic and optimistic turning toward must be that of a trust-ing child. My three-year-old son has a crazy enthusiastic and optimistic trust in me. He will let me throw him fifteen feet in the air over concrete knowing that I will catch him. When I do, he looks up at me and says, "Again!" I often think, "If my son has that much trust in his father, how much more should I trust my Father in heaven?" I bet if we can get our-selves to take some conversational risks, put ourselves out there, and trust in God, we will experience something just as exhilarating as my three-year-old flying fifteen feet in the air. And after we take these conversational risks, we'll look up at God and say, "Again, again!"

Here is one more divine opportunity from David to highlight the type of observant, obedient, and optimistic responsiveness we should all pursue. This is another great example of how he enthusiastically turns toward God with a "Yes, and..."

> I spend my summers visiting with family and preaching on occasional weekends throughout the Midwest. Former students of mine from Central Bible College and North Central Univer-sity, who are now pastors at various churches across the country, will invite me to come and speak to their congregation. In the summer of 2006, I was in a Midwest city preaching at one of these churches.
>
> This particular day, I was halfway through my sermon when three young women walked in the back of the church and sat down. They caught my eye because they weren't dressed for

church. Each of them was wearing heavy black makeup, black clothing, and Gothic jewelry. As I preached they really weren't interested in anything that I had to say. In fact, they talked and laughed throughout the remainder of the service. When I noticed their actions, I prayed in my heart that something that I said would pull on their heart and they would join me at the altar.

At the end of the service, when I did the altar call for those that would like to pray or accept Jesus, they just sat back and continued to laugh and talk. After I finished praying with the others, they were still sitting and waiting around in the back of the church. I figured I would just go back and find out what their story was all about.

As I approached the three young women, one of them said to me, "Dr. Watson, do you remember me?" Typically there was no way I would remember this young woman. She was practically hidden behind heavy black makeup. But as I looked into her eyes, I had one of those divine moments. Humanly speaking, there was no way to recognize this young woman. Again, I looked into her eyes, and experienced a divine opportunity. I recognized her. She was a student of mine from Central Bible College, and just like that her name, the class that I had with her, and where she sat in the classroom popped into my head.

Those moments are awesome to me, because God is about to do something. You don't know what He is about to do, you just know that this unconditional love is working. And so she asked me, "Do you remember me? Do you remember my name?" I said to her, "You're Sarah from my Personal Evangelism class, and you sat in the third row from the back."

She got a puzzled look on her face. You know, divine opportunities will puzzle you. When it's not in your control, in fact, when it's out of your control, God can do so much more. She looked at me and said, "You remember me!" And at this point she started to cry.

The two girls who were with her got up and ran for cover. They didn't want to have anything to do with what was happening. They didn't understand how God works and what God was doing in this moment. It was something so special between the three of us—Sarah, myself, and God—and the other girls just took off.

Sarah then told me, "We were driving around the city when I heard an advertisement on the radio that you were going to be at this church speaking today. For some reason, I found myself doing a U-turn. The girls who were with me, asked, 'What are you doing?' And I told them that I had to go and hear this man speak today." Sarah said, "Really, they were here to mock me."

Sarah continued, "I went to Central Bible College and I had a horrible experience. The other students rejected me, made fun of me, and there was no one there at the time who encouraged me. It seemed like most people didn't even know that I existed. I thought to myself, 'If this is what it's all about, I don't want to have anything to do with it.' So I left the school and I left God." Sarah continued, "Just now though, when you said my name, something happened in me that I've been longing for!" Then she asked, "Will you pray with me?"

Excitedly, we went down to the altar and had a marvelous time with God. Then we went back and she was about to leave when she said something that has stuck with me all these years since. It was so impactful on my life that I wrote it down. She said, "Dr. Watson, there are a lot of people out there just like me, who need to experience God firsthand. There are too many people living on secondhand experiences of other people. I needed this firsthand experience with God. I needed to be reminded that God Himself really does care about me personally. That is what I experienced today!"

In the words of my three-year-old, "Again, again, God. Again!" What a powerful closing line from Sarah: "there are a lot of people out there who need to experience God firsthand. There are too many people living on the secondhand experiences of other people." These people need to be reminded that God Himself really does care about them personally. How about you? Are you living off the secondhand divine opportunity experiences of others? Do you need to be reminded that God cares about you personally?

This is what risk taking and optimistic obedience are all about. Both Sarah and David responded to God's promptings with optimistic obedience. Sarah responded to the radio announcement and David responded to the presence of these young women. If you can hone your spiritual abilities to recognized God's promptings and accept those personal challenges, then you will be blown away by the firsthand experience you can have with God. The stories in this book are amazing and motivating to read, but there needs to come a time when you make a commitment and take action to experience these divine opportunities for yourself.

Discussion Questions

1. What is the hardest, most challenging, aspect about engaging in divine opportunities?
2. What are three back-pocket questions that could turn conversation in a momentum-building direction?
3. Who comes to mind when you think about people who enthusiastically turn toward others in conversation? How do these people's relationships differ from those that rarely or never enthusiastically turn toward others?

Part Three

Discovering Your Divine Destiny

God wants you to get where God wants you to go,
more than you want to get where God wants you to go.
And He's awfully good at getting us there.

—Mark Batterson

We serve a God who knows the number of hairs on our head and the number of stars in the universe. I realize that knowing the number of hairs on some people's head isn't as impressive as others, but come on…God has an insane, mind-boggling micro and macro view over all things from the smallest single cell to the vastness of the galaxies. And that God, the one and only, passionately desires a personal relationship with each one of us. That's crazy awesome. What a relational God we serve. God knows the intimate details of each of our lives. He knows the insecurities that we struggle with but never share with anyone else. He knows all the ways we have been hurt and helped by others. He knows every struggle and every success that has taken place in our lifetime. And He knows how each of those interweaves and interconnects to one another, making each of our lives a one-of-a-kind adventure here on earth.

One of the best parts of doing this research on divine opportunities has been hearing people's stories of how God connected them to others in conversation that was incredibly timely, impactful, and unique. It was as if God put them into conversation with a particular person, not any ole random person, but a particular person who they were able to connect with in a way that few people could have. Of the divine opportunities that I have heard, there are a good number of them that involve stories of two people coming together over a common bond where the pain of one person's past was repurposed for the benefit of the other. God seemed to link two people together in conversation where one person who struggled with an issue in the past was getting to walk another through that same issue in the present. God was uniquely interweaving the lives of people for the purpose of emotional healing.

Hearing all the divine opportunities of others has helped me realize that every person is walking around with unheard and untold stories of pain, disappointment, and distress. Part of our job as Christians is to be mindful of this and to remain on the lookout for opportunities to explore the unheard and untold stories of others. When we do it opens us up to being used by God to care for and comfort those in need, and sometimes God matches us up with someone who is struggling with the same need that we have battled ourselves. And there is nothing more special than God repurposing the pain from our past to the emotional benefit of another in the present. As odd as it may seem, I believe that is the fulfillment of one's divine destiny; to connect with someone in a way that no one else could.

Low-Points

This is why I have started using an assignment in my interpersonal communication class called the Low-Point Pain Funnel Conversation. For this particular assignment, I ask students to have a conversation with three different people to explore a low-point in each of their lives. I instruct the students to follow three simple steps. Step one, set aside time for a personal conversation in a private setting with each of the three people; step two, simply open up the conversation by asking, "Would you mind sharing with me a low-point that you have been through or are currently going through in your life?"; and step three, be quiet and listen closely.

It has been shocking to read through the reports of these conversations, which are kept anonymous. Some semesters I have forty students who will have three conversations each, so when I sit down to read them I end up with a window into the lives of a 120 different low-points. There hasn't been a semester that has gone by that I didn't cry as I read through these. The first time I did this assignment I didn't know what to expect, so I was caught off guard as I read about abortions, miscarriages, deaths of parents, deaths of siblings, physical abuse, sexual abuse, emotional abuse, and bullying. You name it, I've read about it in this assignment. It was a major wakeup call for myself and my students in regard to how many people are walking around with a heavy burden that they are carrying.

You Never Asked

Another surprising aspect of this assignment has been the reports from students as they share something to this effect, "I've known this friend for years now, and I had no idea that they struggled with _____." It's crazy how many of our closest family members, friends, neighbors, and colleagues are walking around with serious burdens that we are clueless about. In fact, this realization caused one of my students, Sofia, to reflect with the following sentiment:

> I recently started thinking about that saying, "You never asked," and I have grown a large distaste for it. I have started to hear it far more regularly than ever before. For example, my stepmom's uncle is always over at our house and I was so confused as to why. My perspective of him changed the other day when I was talking to him and he told me about his two children dying at birth and his fiancé dying from cancer just months later. He said that by hanging around my family he gets the chance to be a part of the family he never had the opportunity to enjoy. I said, "I didn't know any of this about you." He looked at me and said, "Well, how would you? You've never asked." Since becoming aware of this phrase I hear it everywhere and my heart breaks a little more each time.

I agree with Sofia, this is a phrase that we are likely to hear more and more often, and our hearts should be shaken by this each time. It implies that we have grown so accustomed to making small talk that we never take the time to explore deeper issues with people. Society is rapidly heading in a direction that leads us more and more into isolation, and makes it more and more awkward to ask personal questions that explore difficult experiences in people's lives. Most people have accepted silence as they stand in public lines, TV watching has become privatized as we view shows individually on our computers and iPads, and to ask a deep or personal question of someone is seen as nosy, prying, and none of our business.

People's personal stories are very much our business as Christians (within reason of course). Finding the right time and the right place to ask insightful questions of others is an art. It provides you with a window into the lives of others, and often that window leads to a place of deep connection, empathy, and relational development. As you will see in these final chapters, sharing something personal of one's self can free others up to do the same and create a unique moment of connection. Asking genuine questions of others can fulfill a desire in others as they have been longing for the moment when someone would take an interest in their struggles that exist below their social surface. And it's incredible how God uses those people who are open, vulnerable, and willing to take a relational risk.

Let's develop a similar distaste as Sofia for the phrase "you never asked," and let's make ourselves available to God so He can open our eyes to our divine destiny as we minister to people in and through the low-points of life that are shared with us in divine opportunities.

Chapter 9

Vulnerability Breeds Vulnerability

*Finally, all of you, live in harmony with
one another; be sympathetic, love as brothers,
be compassionate and humble.*

—1 Peter 3:8

On several occasions in the Bible, God instructs us to be humble. He warns us not to boast, but to humble ourselves in our thoughts, words, and actions. I take 1 Peter 3:8 to be a prescription for harmonious living. If we express sympathy, compassion, humility, and brotherly and sisterly love, then we will find ourselves living in harmony with those around us—most importantly, with God.

In this chapter we will take a close look at what happens in conversation when we express, rather than suppress, humility. One of the ways that we can express humility is through vulnerability; thus, sharing the authentic versions of ourselves and our stories with others. Later in this chapter, you will read two divine opportunities that resulted from the expression of humility through vulnerability, which God used to break two conversations and relationships wide open.

Vulnerability

Researcher, professor, and author Dr. Brene Brown has become a well-known advocate for vulnerability. With more than twenty million views of her TED Talk on vulnerability and *New York Times* bestselling books on vulnerability, she has clearly found a topic that resonates with people. In fact, her research and writing on vulnerability ties in with the idea that vulnerability breeds vulnerability. When you have the courage to express humility through vulnerability in conversations and relationships, then you'll often receive humility and vulnerability back in kind. This notion has been essential in many divine opportunity stories that I have heard over the years. Here are several quotes from Dr. Brene Brown that help us define and understand this position of vulnerability and what role it may play in God repurposing the pain from our past for the benefit of another in the present.

> We cultivate love when we allow our most vulnerable and powerful selves to be deeply seen and known, and when we honor the spiritual connection that grows from that offering with trust, respect, kindness and affection.
>
> Authenticity is a collection of choices that we have to make every day. It's about the choice to show up and be real. The choice to be honest. The choice to let our true selves be seen.
>
> I now see how owning our story and loving ourselves through that process is the bravest thing that we will ever do.
>
> Imperfections are not inadequacies; they are reminders that we're all in this together.

The call to be humble and vulnerable is no easy task. Most people associate humility and vulnerability with weakness, meekness, and feebleness. Dr. Brown has made it her mission to flip this thinking to illustrate that humility and vulnerability demand the opposite. Instead, humility and vulnerability require great strength, courage, and confidence. This has ultimately made Dr. Brown famous in our modern YouTube culture. Not to take anything away from Dr. Brown, because her work is incredible and she has a fantastic sense of humor, but some people don't realize that she was not the first person to acknowledge the strength and courage in humility and vulnerability. The Bible actually established this line of thinking over 2,000 years ago (but, whatever).

From a Christian perspective, there is such biblical depth behind humility and vulnerability. I will merely scratch the surface in this chapter to highlight a few strategic ways we can think about, embrace, and utilize vulnerability to the benefit of divine opportunities. I'd first like to start with an example of this from Shannon, a hairstylist who lives in the Midwest. In Shannon's divine opportunity she owned her story of imperfection, expressed humility through vulnerability, and thus allowed God to shine through in her authentic testimony of His saving grace.

> I have a long-term client of mine, of seven years, and about six months ago she was scheduled for an appointment. She was supposed to come in midday for a highlight. When she arrived for her appointment she had brought with her a seventeen-year-old girl who was looking really rough around the edges—like wearing pajamas and a blanket in public kind of rough. This woman asked if the girl could also get in right after her. She explained that she had taken this young girl into her home because her family life was very troubled. In fact, this young girl was already struggling with alcoholism and sexual abuse at seventeen years old. The woman was wanting to do something nice for her before school started to make her feel good about herself.
>
> Normally, there is no way I could squeeze her in even if I wanted to. I'm booked all day long and all week long. I've been blessed with a great group of clients who keep me busy year around. It's great, but it doesn't allow for walk-ins or any flexibility in scheduling. Also, my clients don't cancel their appointments; they know that if they cancel it will be another month before they can get back in to see me. However, on this particular day, the client scheduled immediately after her had called five minutes before she walked through the door and cancelled her appointment. We were able to fit this young girl in, when normally there would have been zero chance to do so.
>
> After I highlighted the woman's hair, she asked if she could leave and run some errands during the girl's appointment. At first, I was a bit surprised by the request because she had just spent several minutes talking about how out of control she was and how she couldn't get her to do anything she asked. You don't usually leave those kinds of teens alone with others. But I could easily tell that this young girl was broken and needed some love.

I told her that would be fine, and that I would take care of her. The woman warned me, "She won't talk to you, so you can just do her hair and I'll be back to pick her up."

Well, that young seventeen-year-old girl sat down in my chair and I got to spend an hour and half with her. Just based on what little information my client had shared about her, I could quickly recognize several similarities between our life stories. When I was younger I struggled with abuse and alcoholism. In fact, when I was her age I got pregnant with my daughter. And just a couple years ago I had gotten into serious trouble for drinking and driving, so I was years into my recovery with AA. It was amazing to see how God had prepared me and trained me to mentor this young girl throughout her appointment. I was able to anticipate what she was thinking and feeling before she ever said anything at all. I knew how to connect with her rather than push her away in conversation. As I opened up about my story, I could tell that she became more comfortable opening up about hers.

She went on to share her complete brokenness. She laid it all out there, how she grew up in an alcoholic home with sexual abuse and no rules. She grew up in a home where there was no love and no attention. You see, most people who deal with substance and sexual abuse lose their self-worth. More than anything, she needed someone to listen to her. But she also needed someone to let her know that she wasn't alone. This was my unique contribution.

Out of all the hair stylists that she could have gone to see, I was the only one who could completely relate to what she was going through during that phase of her life. God gave me an opportunity to share my experience and show her that there was a way out. He allowed me to love on her for an hour and a half and show her that she was worth something and I let her know that she was not alone. For an hour and a half she was able to feel like she wasn't crazy. But this wasn't the end. I got to show her, through my own life story, that her life was just as redeemable. If nothing else, I got to give her a little hope.

I gave her my number and told her that if she ever needed anything to just give me a call. Unfortunately, several months had passed and I hadn't heard from her, so I figured that the she was never going to call—there was never going to be anything that happened from this. Then I ran into the woman who was taking care of her and she said, "Oh, she's out of control, she's back with her family and she's still a mess." At that point, I figured I had already had my chance, I had put it all out there. God gave me that one opportunity and I did what I could. Perhaps that was it and I would never get another opportunity with her.

Well, this story goes a little all over the place, but I went to an AA meeting a couple of weeks ago and I was visiting with a few others when a guy came up to me and said, "One of my friends, who's been in the program for about thirty years, has this daughter who is just a mess and we're trying to get her some help. We wanted to know if we could have her call you? I just think that she'd really like you." I figured even though I couldn't help the other girl at the salon, that perhaps things might be different with this guy's daughter. I told him that I would be happy to talk with her and I gave him my number to pass along.

Just a couple of days ago I received a voicemail from the friend's daughter. As I listened to the message, I realized that this young woman was the same one who sat in my chair months ago. God reconnected us—He keeps putting this girl into my life. I'm praying this is another chance to reach her, connect with her, and help her. Hopefully, this is another opportunity to show her love and God's light and bring it out of her in any way that I can.

Through this girl I have been able to see a part of me that I have left behind and I have been able to see where I might have been at that age. God shows us just as much in divine opportunities about ourselves as He does with the people we are ministering to. I have been able to see that God can use all the horrible things in my life to help other people in those same situations. I can look at it from a place of healing now. I get to share with her my hope and experience with how God has changed and redeemed my life.

This is a great example of how vulnerability breeds vulnerability. Shannon explicitly said, "As I opened up about my story, I could tell that she became more comfortable opening up about hers." There is a *huge* lesson in that statement for all of us. If you want to open yourself up to divine opportunities like this, it may require putting yourself in a vulnerable position from time to time through the telling of your own imperfect story.

Keep in mind that "imperfections are not inadequacies; they are reminders that we're all in this together." We are all imperfect. Imperfection is inevitable in this life. The key is to express that God redeems us all and makes us perfect through the sacrifice of His Son Jesus Christ. That sacrifice makes us whole despite any imperfections. I've learned the hard lesson that being imperfect is not the problem, walking around as if I am perfect is. The truth of the matter is that imperfections draw people in and perfection pushes people away.

Okay—Not Okay

The Okay—Not Okay principle used in psychology further highlights this need for humility through vulnerability in conversation. The principle is based on the idea that the vast majority of the population is constantly seeking to feel "okay" about themselves.[62] Feeling "okay" about oneself means that someone is comfortable in their own skin, comfortable with who they are, and confident in their abilities, intelligence, and achievements. However, many people feel "not okay" about their lives, who they are, what they know, and what they can do, which significantly affects their self-esteem. Thus, people are regularly in pursuit of ways to make themselves feel "okay."

The primary way that people seek to feel "okay" about themselves is by identifying other people who are worse off than themselves. Essentially, people are on a scavenger hunt to find someone they can look at and say, "I've got it bad, but not as bad as _____." "I've messed up, but I haven't messed up as bad as _____." These other people's "not okayness" makes them feel more "okay" about themselves. This same idea applies even if people can find one thing in someone else's life that puts the other person in a "not okay" position and puts themselves in the "okay" position.

For example, the somewhat nerdy math major gets to tutor the beloved college football quarterback. The quarterback is put in the "not okay" position during tutoring, and the math major gets to feel more "okay" as a result. The same applies when the marriage expert shares with couples attending a marriage conference that they themselves have a "high maintenance marriage" that requires work. In this case, the marriage expert shares some level of being "not okay" in order to allow those in attendance to feel more "okay," and thus more comfortable in that learning environment.

This may seem silly, but I am suggesting that we use this Okay—Not Okay principle to our advantage to relate with others and create opportunities for moments of connection. Here are three thoughts for using this principle of Okay—Not Okay in relationship-enhancing ways.

Unintended Consequences of an Overly "Okay" Appearance

First is a warning to be mindful of the unintentional ways that you present yourself as perfect, well put together, unflawed, and very much "okay." Believe it or not, but many people do this without much thought toward realizing what sort of impact their unflawed version of themselves has on others. Think about it: if most people are seeking to identify imperfections of others to make themselves feel better, and all you let people see is the unflawed side of yourself, this will ultimately make them feel worse about themselves. Thus, it may push them away, and likely make them feel bitter and slighted by your extreme appearance of being "okay."

The Tim Tebow effect. This is why so many people love to see Tim Tebow fail in some aspect of life. At first glance, Tebow seems to have it all, he's well put together, he's buff as all get-out, he's handsome, and he seems to have deserved and undeserved success that drives his "okayness" through the roof. This makes people (primarily non-Christians) feel inferior and second-rate. His seemingly successful and perfect life makes people feel all the worse about their own. Oddly, these people experienced a euphoric high when Tebow struggled to get resigned by an NFL team because it reminded them that he was human and they gained some satisfaction knowing he wasn't perfect. I truly believe that these unintended consequences were at the root of the media frenzy and non-Christian backlash Tebow experienced.

Well, guess what? This doesn't just apply to Tim Tebow. This applies to you and me as well. Think about this in terms of people whom you follow on Facebook. There are probably people whom, when you read their posts on Facebook, it makes you feel better or worse about your own circumstances. This has actually become a bit of a problem in that most people's Facebook page consists of their Top 10 list of great, wonderful, exciting things they did for the week. That in and of itself is not the problem. The problem arises when people leave out all of their Not Top 10 experiences for the week (I'm taking a page out of the *Sports Center* playbook). Thus, the only perception people have of them is their awesomeness, and the unintended consequence is that it sometimes makes people feel less awesome about themselves.

Sports Center is really on to something here. Originally, ESPN started out with just the Top 10 Plays, and then they realized that viewers enjoyed seeing the Not Top 10 Plays just as much. As a result, the Top 10 Plays allow us to marvel over the top athletic feats of the day, and the Not Top 10 Plays allow us to feel good about the fact that even pro golfers will occasionally hit a tee shot that shatters the clubhouse window.

How are you, as a Christian, impacted by the Tim Tebow effect? Do you only share things online and in-person that make you look good? Do you hide and cover up your imperfections, insecurities, and embarrassing moments? If so, there might be unintended consequences to this lack of vulnerability in the presence of others. Without even realizing it, you might be experiencing the Tebow effect with non-Christian friends of yours who are turned away by your appearance of perfection because it further reminds them of their own imperfections. You may even have non-Christian friends who are just waiting for the moment that you screw up, and they finally get their finger-pointing moment to spot another hypocritical Christian.

The point of the Tebow effect (which unfortunately was completely out of Tebow's control) is that we should be sensitive to moments and opportunities to let others know that we are just as imperfect as everyone else. We are just as much a work-in-progress as the next person, and the only reason for our "okayness" is because of Jesus Christ. We have to be okay with the fact that not everyone will appreciate that. Just look at Tebow—he attributed every success to Christ and rejected all self-praise and people still hated him because they couldn't help but feel less "okay" about themselves in the wake of his success.

Here's one more example of unintended consequences stemming from faking an overly "okay" appearance. In my first year of full-time teaching at Azusa Pacific University, I was teaching three new course preps that I hadn't taught before, transitioning to full-time faculty status, and adapting to life in California with a wife and one kiddo. To be honest, I was insecure, lacking confidence, struggling in the classroom, and willing to do whatever needed to cover up my "not okayness." Instead of sharing those vulnerabilities with the students, I decided to take the approach of "fake it till I make it." I dressed as nice as possible, I graded tough, I took my lectures seriously, I kept strict policies with the students, and I joked little. The result of that first year was horrific. Many students disliked me and weren't afraid to say it. You can check www.ratemyprofessor.com if you don't believe me. My presentation of unauthentic "okayness" just caused the students to think that I was uncaring, arrogant, and pompous. As Christians, we can unintentionally do this same thing online and in-person. For some reason, we think we need to present this cover-up of "okayness" to others, which ultimately leads to a pompous interpretation.

The unintended consequence of trying to appear put-together, confident, and perfect in the classroom was a difficult pill to swallow when I read many of the end of semester reviews. It wasn't until I settled into my classes and figured out what the heck I was doing that I gave myself permission to be silly, cut loose, and laugh at myself in the classroom. When I let my guard down, students really started to warm up to me. The more I shared bits and pieces of my own imperfect relational, academic, and professional career, the more I seemed to bond with the students. Since letting some of my "not okayness" out of the box, students seem more open to sharing about their lives and seeking out personal connections with me outside the classroom. Of course, this disclosure of imperfection has to be done in moderation and in appropriate ways.

Knowing this, I now strategically set myself up to appear "not okay" and thus allow the students to feel more "okay" around me. I'll let you in on a secret example. Each semester, I will randomly pick a day to intentionally use my wife's hand lotion before going to teach, and then at the start of class I'll say something like, "Before we start I just want to let you know that if anyone catches a whiff of something that smells extra fruity, it's likely me. On my way out of the house this morning I used what I thought was unscented hand lotion. Turns out, it was my wife's *very* scented, Passion Fruit hand lotion." Then, we all share a quick laugh, and I go on to talk about research methodology. Of course, now I've blown my cover and I'll have to come up with new "not okay" humor for bonding purposes.

Strategically Sharing Our Imperfections

This leads to the second thought of the Okay—Not Okay principle, which is that we need to be strategic about the various ways that we can genuinely, and sometimes humorously, share the realities of our imperfections with others. When we share our own imperfections, we allow others to accept their own imperfections. The unintended consequence of this approach is that both people gain feelings of being "okay" through mutual acceptance of being "not okay" together. In these moments of vulnerability, people realize that they are not alone in these imperfections, and it typically comes in the form of a therapeutic conversation.

For example, I have observed that many people comment on how funny my wife is on Facebook and how much they enjoy her posts. The reason being, she is not afraid to share her Not Top 10 moments right along with her Top 10 for the week. She is willing to regularly post the ridiculous and embarrassing moments she has in life.

One time she shared that when she was checking out at Target she received a bunch of $1 off coupons. One of the coupons was for a $1 off at Starbucks. As she was walking by the Starbucks inside Target, she decided to give the coupon to this woman standing in line. When she got back to the car, loaded up the kids, and looked at the remaining coupons, she realized that she still had the $1 off Starbucks coupon and that she had accidently given the woman a $1 off Huggies diapers.

My wife also posts some difficult realities of having children. She's willing to laugh at herself and admit that she's not a perfect parent and that our kids aren't always perfect angels. She's even willing to be vulnerable and open about her post baby body, stretch marks and all. This display of "not okayness" actually makes other moms feel better about their bodies, parenting, and kids' behavior.

Thus, my wife's vulnerability breeds vulnerability. This has resulted in other women opening up to her about their own insecurities with their bodies, parenting, and kids. Her humility has led to great conversations with other moms where they can laugh, cry, and complain about their common struggles. My wife has experienced some wonderful moments that were unintended consequences of her ability to accept and embrace "not okay" aspects of herself. Ultimately, God uses the "not okay" aspects of our lives just as much as He uses the "okay" aspects. And if we allow ourselves to discern and select appropriate times to share those "not okay" aspects with others, I think we will be amazed at the work God does in those relationships.

TMI vs. NEI

Here's one final thought about using vulnerability to our advantage to create conversational opportunities. There is great risk in providing not enough information (NEI) rather than providing too much information (TMI) in conversation with others. One shorthand expression most of us are familiar with is TMI. Somebody overshares too much detail and we jokingly say, "TMI." Well, I think there are just as many times when we suppress, instead of express, vulnerability and humility, which leads to an error on the other end of the spectrum of NEI. In fact, many of the missed opportunities people have shared with me involved God convicting them with the thought of NEI. As you think about these principles and unintended consequences of our communication, or lack thereof, you may begin to recognize opportunities where you failed to share some vulnerable aspect or detail of your life story and missed an opportunity to bond with someone over a shared life struggle.

Moderation between TMI and NEI is going to be lifelong battle for all of us. It requires tremendous awareness, sensitivity, and spiritual discernment to decide when to speak up and when to remain silent, when to share our successes and when to share our struggles. When you experience this dilemma, in regard to risking self-disclosure, I encourage you to hit the pause button, send up a prayer, and allow God to lead you. Obviously, you don't want to share a deeply personal story with someone that will take it, twist it, and misuse it. But you also don't want to pass up an opportunity to share details of your "not okay" testimony with someone who desperately needs to hear it. Because, if you do, you could be passing up an opportunity to rescue someone from self-shame. Don't rob someone of your testimony of how God has redeemed your life and brought you out of your insecurities because of societal fears, worries, or concerns of TMI.

If you feel like something is borderline TMI, here is a quick interpersonal check-in you can do to better gauge those feelings. Simply ask the other person for permission to share. Usually, a question like, "Would it be okay if I shared my story with you?" or "This might be awkward or uncomfortable, but can I ask a personal question?" will do fine. By getting permission, you avoid forcing your emotional story or personal testimony on them, and they welcome the conversation. You can also pause occasionally during the conversation and make sure they are still onboard with the disclosure. Sometimes once the gates open on vulnerability, either side can go too far, and it becomes too much too soon. It's important to be spiritually and emotionally sensitive to the other person and their verbal and nonverbal reactions to your disclosure.

Below is a tough but beautiful example of a divine opportunity that resulted from Sally, a therapist, embracing her vulnerability and responding to the NEI conviction from God. This is an example of a powerful connection over shared "imperfections," and how God repurposes the pain from "not okay" experiences of the past to bring about "okayness" in the present.

> This divine opportunity was between myself—I'm a therapist—and a client of mine, a young woman in her twenties. There seemed to be several unique circumstances and overlaps in our two stories that were so distinct it truly stood out as God ordained.

The first "coincidence" was how this young woman found me to begin with as she was searching for Christian therapists. It's a bit random, but if you put in just the right search criteria in Google, I'm the only therapist who shows up in my area as a Christian therapist. If you search Saint Paul, fully written out, my name doesn't come up. If you search St Paul, without a period, my name doesn't come up either. You will get a whole bunch of other therapists, but you won't get me. But if you search St. Paul, with a period, you get me and nobody else. It's just the way they set up their search engine. I meant to call them and correct it, but I have had so many other things going on I never did.

Well, as it turns out, this young lady came to see me and she thought I was the only one there was. Turns out, there's a lot of other choices, but because of the way she searched I was the only choice. I explained it to her when she got there, "You have other choices. I don't want you to think this is your only choice." But she was comfortable with me and didn't care to continue her search. That was the first unique circumstance that caused me to reflect on all the ways God set up this moment.

This beautiful young lady was seeking a therapist because she had been having panic attacks and anxiety. She was having a hard time coping because there were many triggers in her life. As she shared her life events and experiences with me, I quickly identified several similarities between the two of us. That's not necessarily all that unusual. That happens—that's part of why I'm a counselor.

In therapy I always start with something small and then work up to bigger and bigger issues and triggers in people's lives. At this point, we were on our tenth session, and were working on one of biggest sources of pain. She was date raped; although she didn't understand that she was date raped prior to our therapy. She was so confused by the whole experience that she couldn't come to terms with what had happened exactly; she didn't know if it was date rape or if she had consented.

When something's really painful, you feel all the emotion and all that anxiety again. You don't know what to do with it so you push it back again. You never stop and entertain it long enough to figure out what you know. The type of therapy that I do helps your brain bring up the information that it does know but doesn't know how to process.

For the first time, she was able to share her story with more detail and analysis than ever before. At the time of the event, she was a junior in college and she had gone to a party with her girlfriends. Her and her girlfriends were all virgins and they were all committed to remaining virgins and saving themselves until they were married. This group of girls had all gone to this party together. There was a guy at the party that she had dated before, and they had mutually broken up some time earlier. Next thing she knew she was waking up in his apartment realizing that they had sex. She got up to go to the bathroom, and she was upset. She came back, and he said, "I don't know why you're so upset." She said, "Well, you know, what happened? I don't even know what happened." He said, "Well, you begged me to do it." She was very confused; she didn't understand how that could be true.

So she started to think maybe there was some part of her that wanted this. All this was still inside her, after all this time, and she was still not married. She was still thinking, "Maybe there's this part of me that's dangerous, this part of me that will do something like this when I have a drink." She had one glass of wine the night of the incident, so she started to think she lost control—at least that's what he told her. Her brain was so confused at the time that it didn't know what to do with that information.

As we were processing, I helped her stop and notice some things that she hadn't allowed herself to identify before. "So you were in a purity group and this was really important to you to not have sex until marriage." She said, "Yeah, that's true." I said, "Just notice that." Then we'd continue, and she began to realize, "There's something fishy about this." Of course, you and I realize it, but when something like this happens to you, you get so confused that you can't quite capture the details and the big picture simultaneously. The big piece that I think she was missing, and that I realized as I was sitting there listening to her, was that I thought she was drugged.

She knew him so it was hard for her to believe that he would do something like that. Then she started remembering, "Now that I think about it, he and his group of friends played a game that counted how many virgins they can have sex with." It was like a baseball thing where everyone you got, you got a new base. Previously, she hadn't connected all the dots before.

The big piece of the equation that she didn't know about was the date rape drug. There's not a lot of information about it; it's still quite ambiguous. Few people are explaining it to others because even the people who have been drugged don't really understand what happened to them. But I knew because several years back I met this nice young attorney. We began talking, and he was representing a seventeen-year-old who was being brought to court because fifteen girls were accusing him of giving them a date rape drug. As I was listening to him, I was just getting more and more curious about this whole date rape drug thing because this was the first time I'd ever heard of it.

I asked questions like, "How would this happen fifteen times? Why didn't they catch him after the first time?" He said, "Well, it's an amnesiac. The victim doesn't necessarily know they've been drugged. The victim is aware enough when it's happening to realize what they've done, but they don't really know why they did it. The victim basically loses volition. They are awake, so on some level they think they have potentially consented by participating, but really they don't have the ability to say yes or no."

I gave her that information and she continued to process. Then she replied, "Well, if this is what date rape drugs do, I still don't understand why so few people know about this?" It's like she couldn't believe that it was really true. But I knew.

I felt this nudge and realized that this was a divine opportunity. I realized that I had to share with her that the same thing happened to me. I was also drugged and date raped in college. It was a really weird feeling because it was very risky. You don't do that as a therapist. You're not ever supposed to tell your own story. But I had to be faithful to the nudging, so I told her. I let her know that it was ten years later before I realized what had happened to me. I too thought that somehow I had this dangerous side to myself, because I had also decided I was going to save myself for marriage. And I had the same reaction, shame, and memory suppression as her.

I told her about my experience, and then asked her, "I'd like you to consider the possibility that you were drugged, and someone really took advantage of you." When she started putting all these pieces together, she was able to see, "All this time, I've been holding this against myself, and it wasn't me. I didn't do that. It was done to me. I had to do what I had to do to survive."

Then she had to go through the whole being mad at God thing, which takes a while to get through. She said, "Why would God allow something like this?" I said, "I don't know, but I can tell you that in this moment, I can see some good coming out of what happened to me because I'm sitting here telling you, and you're now able to have some healing from this." She's probably going to have the opportunity to share her story at some point as well. Why do terrible things happen? I don't have an answer for that, but God uses them—they're not in isolation—and that's pretty powerful.

It was pretty cool to see how God can take the most wounded parts of ourselves and use them to help heal other people. You don't see it coming either. I never would have thought I was ever going to share that. But it was so obviously a God-appointed opportunity. Both of us recognized this was a God appointment by all the similarities and overlapping details between our two life stories. So when I said, "Look, this happened to me too," then she really thought, "God put me here to hear that from you." It was pretty cool.

Disclosure Risks

While there is incredible power in the act of personal disclosure and the sharing of a vulnerable testimony, we also need to acknowledge some of the risks of self-disclosure. The basic risks for the one doing the self-disclosing is that their personal vulnerabilities could be twisted, misused, and exploited by the wrong recipients. Unfortunately, there are people who may use that information against us or share it with others outside of the private confines of the conversation.

On the other side, we need to avoid burdening others with inappropriate disclosures. For example, I have heard of professors oversharing their personal marital struggles with their students in the classroom that didn't fit the nature of the student-professor relationship. Thus, it put the students in an awkward and uncomfortable position that they didn't sign up for. To calculate for such risks, prayerfully consider when, where, and with whom you are sharing your vulnerabilities. A quick assessment of appropriateness, context, and relational fit can go a long way to avoid potential disclosure risks for both parties involved.

Discussion Questions

1. Who is someone in your life that has effectively shared their imperfections with you in a way that made you feel closer and more connected? What can you learn from that person and experience?
2. What are a few of your imperfections that God may prompt you to share with others in the future? Who might benefit from hearing about your "not okay" moments?
3. Who is someone in your friend group that may be impacted by the Tim Tebow Effect as a result of sharing only their Top 10 List on social media without any posts about their Not Top 10? How might this impact their relationships with others?
4. How might you personally be impacted by the Tim Tebow Effect with your non-Christian friends, coworkers, or family members?

Chapter 10
Match Made in Heaven

*Praise be to the God and Father of our Lord Jesus
Christ, the Father of compassion and the God of all
comfort, who comforts us in all our troubles, so that we
can comfort those in any trouble with the comfort we
ourselves have received from God.*

—*2 Corinthians 1:3–4*

"So that we can comfort those in any trouble with the comfort we ourselves have received from God." This is one of those verses that has been brought to light in a new way for me by several divine opportunity stories I've heard over the years. One regular occurring theme that I have noticed is how often God uses the pain from one person's past to minister to someone going through a similar source of pain in the present.

You've already read a few stories that highlight this source of divine comfort through the examples provided by Sally (comforting a fellow victim of date rape) and Shannon (comforting a fellow victim of physical, sexual, and emotional abuse, and alcoholism), as well as Larry (comforting a mother struggling with her son's diagnosis of leukemia from the source of his pain in losing his first wife to leukemia). In each of those three examples—Sally,

Shannon, and Larry—they all comfort those in trouble with the comfort they received from God.

In this chapter we'll take a closer look at these divine matches where God brings two people together—one in need and one to provide comfort for the need—in a way that reminds them both of the greatness and goodness of God's mercy. The first example of this comes from Elissa, a thirty-year-old mother and church volunteer, whose story is a modern illustration of 2 Corinthians 1:3–4.

Around the time of the divine opportunity, the youth pastor at my church had been asking me to volunteer as a small group leader in the high school ministry. In fact, he had been regularly asking me to do this for a couple of years, each time telling him no. I had twins, I was really busy, and it's just was not a good time for me. I really didn't give him the time of day. He asked, I said no, and we were done. Not one part of me wanted to go back to high school ministry. It had been about four years since I had been involved in any type of youth ministry and I was okay with that.

Then one summer morning, I was at our church helping to check-in kids at VBS when I ran into this youth pastor once again. This was right before a doctor's appointment for Leah, one of my two-year-old twins. Again he asked if I might consider doing a high school group, and again I said no, and then I went on my way to take Leah to this appointment.

Leah had been seeing a neurologist for several months. I had complications during the birthing process, and Leah had been receiving services of one kind or another since then. Every six months we would meet with a neurologist and they would evaluate her and reassess her. They would usually just tell us that she was delayed, but she was doing better and to continue on with the therapy. So I didn't expect this appointment to be any different.

But this time the neurologist told us that Leah was so far behind that if she didn't start to speak by the time that she was three (she was two and a half at this time) then she would likely never speak. This was a big shock, because six months prior we had been told that she was fine but just needed therapy. To hear that your kid may not ever speak—I had just never even thought of that as an option. Then I thought, "How could this happen?"

With all of her combined developmental delays, the doctors

gave her the diagnosis of moderate to severe autism, which I had not been thinking about—I always just thought that she was delayed because she was a twin and was born prematurely. But now they were telling me she may never speak.

I immediately started wondering if she would ever be loved outside of our family. Would she have friends? Would she get married? Would she drive a car? Would she go to college? Would she live with us for the rest of her life? How would I communicate with her if she doesn't speak? I left that appointment with my daughter and husband and I cried the whole way home.

In that moment, my husband wasn't able to understand what I was thinking and feeling. He wasn't relating with me the way I needed him to. Instead of joining me in mourning, so to speak, he was downplaying it by saying that it would all be okay. Then we told my mom and I still just didn't feel comforted. Then I talked to my friends and they just made me angry. They told me not to worry about it, and that she would grow out of it. It was almost as if my feelings weren't justified. Everyone's reactions were just all the more upsetting, so I didn't tell anyone after that.

I went on YouTube and I starting watching videos of kids with similar needs in therapy situations, and the videos were horrible. The kids were acting like robots. These kids were even older than my daughter, and it just took my breath away. All I could think about was how this could be my life.

The next day I was at church and I ran into the youth pastor again. He was trying to joke around with me, "Did you change your mind? Are you ready to do a high school group?" And I remember snapping at him, "No, you don't know what's going on in my life. My whole world is turning upside down and you want me to do a stupid high school group? I don't have the time or the energy for that! If you knew what was going on in my life, you wouldn't be harassing me to do this. I know you're just kidding. But stop! I have a lot going on and you keep bugging me."

Later that night I felt so desperate for connection, and I remembered this lady from church, her name was Stacy, I knew that she was a teacher who worked with special needs kids, but I didn't know anything else about her. I didn't have her cell phone number, so I messaged her on Facebook and said, "Hey, whenever you have a chance, could I ask you some questions?" She called me back and told me that before she was a special needs teacher, she did the exact type of at home therapy that we needed for Leah. What are the odds that she would have had that exact job? She said she only knew about children with these needs from an education standpoint, and that I should really talk to another mother of a child who has special needs. She said, "You need to find Wendy, this woman at our church, and talk with her."

The next day I ran into Wendy at church, we were both volunteering at VBS, and I asked if I could hear about her story. She said that she would be happy to call me and talk about it later. So, Wendy, whom I was not friends with, called me and we talked for a good hour. I was able to tell her everything about Leah. She listened and she prayed with me over the phone, she knew exactly how I felt and she was able to put it into words. Wendy was able to say out loud exactly how I felt. It really touched me because finally someone understood my fears and anxiety that I now had for my child. This woman had gone through this journey for the last eighteen years.

The reason I think this was a divine opportunity was because this complete stranger was there for me when I needed her. My friends, husband, and mom weren't helpful. My go-to people did not understand, as a mother, what it felt like to have a kid who was diagnosed with autism. It was amazing to connect with Wendy, and she was so generous with her time; she spent an hour with me talking. A week later, her and her husband even came out to our house to meet with me and my husband, and they provided such wisdom and encouragement.

Even now, she still randomly sends me cards with words of encouragement, and I've kept them all. Her words are so full of God's truth. On one of the cards she wrote, "Couples can endure more together, so cling to your husband. Don't push him away because he doesn't know how you're feeling." I thought that was so true. In another card she sent, she wrote a verse from Lamentations, where it talks about how God's mercies are new every morning and that we don't have to have fear over anger, anxiety, or autism. There is nothing that our God can't conquer. Those notes have been so encouraging to me, and the little time that Wendy sat down to write and mail them to me meant so much.

Later on that week I began thinking, "Wendy was there when I needed her. She didn't wait a couple of days to get back to me; she called me later that afternoon. She gave me all the time in the world that I needed to sit and to talk with her and she even prayed with me. She made the time for me. Same with Stacy, the therapist. I talked with her over the phone late at night for an hour. And Stacy has young kids, so for a mother that's a lot to give up that late at night. It was really on my heart that these two women, two strangers, gave themselves to me in a way that I desperately needed. My friends, husband, and mom weren't able to help me the way that these two strangers were able to help me and to speak truth to me and encourage me."

That got me thinking about the youth pastor. Here he was reaching out to me numerous times asking me for help. There was a need in the youth group and no one is filling it. It had been a year and these girls needed a leader and they didn't have one. And I kept telling him no. I thought, "What if Wendy would have said, 'No, I'm sorry, I'm really busy, I can't talk to you right now.' Or what if she had said, 'That's kind of an embarrassing subject for me, I don't like to talk about my kid and his special needs, I want others to think my family is perfect.' What if Stacy would have said, 'Sorry, I have two young kids, I'm too busy for you right now.'" These women heard a little bit of my story and they stopped everything to help me. And here this guy was asking for my help numerous times and I didn't give him the time of day.

Then I really felt that God put it on my heart to think about it, pray about it, and talk to my husband about leading the high school group. And despite what it added to our already crazy schedule, I decided to go ahead and be a small group leader. The first night I showed up was actually that Sunday—all this happened in one week. So that Sunday I started, and who was in my group? The daughter of Wendy, the woman who had talked with me about her special needs son. It was like God was keeping Wendy in my life through her daughter, and everything had come full circle.

Elissa's story blows me away at the powerful outcomes that result from people taking the time to comfort others as they themselves have been comforted by God. Wendy's actions are a beautiful picture of what it means to put others' needs above your own, and to put aside distractions and pour into the life of another person. Wendy's connection with Elissa is a great example of what it looks like to go above and beyond in thoughtful action-oriented comfort.

In chapter 2 I talked about how easy it is to slip into an apathetically-sympathetic lifestyle, where our sympathy exists to the extent that it doesn't require much of us. Here Wendy provides a great example of an active-empathic lifestyle. First, she possesses the ability to be truly empathic and feel what Elissa feels because of her own family struggle. Second, she acts on that empathic opportunity through phone conversations, home visits, and handwritten notes. Wendy truly seizes the opportunity God presents for comforting another's need in the present out of the pain from her own past. And she does so beautifully.

Divine Optimal Matching

The relationship that develops between Elissa and Wendy is exemplary of what I call divine optimal matching. The research on "peer support" and "interventions" often utilizes a theory of optimal matching, which emphasizes the effectiveness of social support provided by people who are familiar with the context of the stress-inducing event and have the ability to share experiential knowledge.[63] The benefits of these relationships are focused around shared experiences, mutual self-disclosure, and collaborative problem solving.[64] As Elissa expresses, there is something magical about the support that is provided by someone who has experienced almost exactly the same struggle the other person is currently going through. These optimal matches for support bring connection, identification, and compassion that isn't possible from an unempathetic outsider.

The theory of optimal matching is the basis for the work of Alcoholics Anonymous (AA). The group is run by recovering alcoholics, and new attendees are mentored by fellow alcoholics. It's nearly impossible for someone who has never struggled with alcoholism to fully understand what an alcoholic is thinking, feeling, and experiencing. Whereas a fellow recovering alcoholic knows exactly how intense those cravings can get, how well-intentioned friends can jeopardize sobriety, and how life stressors can trigger nearly irresistible urges to drink. The AA relationships are another great example of what it means to truly comfort others from a place where they themselves have received comfort. No other relationship will be able to provide that same connection of support, encouragement, and wisdom.

The reason for adding the "divine" to the theory of optimal matching is that time and time again God seems to find unique and creative ways to pair people up with a specific person who can truly speak to the source of pain in another's life. And the timeliness of that pairing seems to come at a breaking point in the person's life where there is a sense of desperation and loss of hope. God's divine optimal matching is something that we need to consider in each of our lives.

These divine opportunities are all around us. There is no source of pain too big or too small that doesn't need to be shared in a divine optimal matching relationship. I have heard of comforting relationships where the source of shared pain included everything from the most severe to the mildest struggles. Here is a short list that is just the tip of the iceberg when it comes to life struggles that could tremendously benefit from a divine optimal match for a timely support intervention:

The loss of a parent, grandparent, sibling, spouse, or child
Drug addictions
Sexual temptations
Struggles with cancer
Dealing with divorce
Struggles following an abortion
Sexual abuse
Bullying and cyber-bullying
Parenting difficulties
Marital affairs
College application rejections
Sexual harassment
Foster parenting
Receiving a demotion at work
ADHD, OCD, or any mental disorder
Experiences of discrimination
Experiences of having a child or sibling with special needs
Suffering a career-ending sports injury
Filing for bankruptcy
Navigating stepfamily dynamics
Struggles following a miscarriage
Child abuse
The loss of a family owned business
Unemployment
Getting cut from a sports team
Transferring schools
Extreme poverty and extreme wealth
Chronic back pain
Failing out of college
Post-partum depression

There is a never-ending list of life struggles people go through where the burden could be significantly lightened through a divine optimal matching relationship like that of Elissa and Wendy's. Every person you meet has gone through a struggle and is currently going through a new one. We will not be lacking for opportunities to engage in these types of divine opportunities. But in order to capitalize on these opportunities we need to thoughtfully consider several questions and prepare our hearts to be ready to respond to the opportunities when they do arise:

What is on your list of past and current life struggles?

How might God be positioning you to minister to someone else who is dealing with something you have already dealt with?

How might God be encouraging you to open up and share your current struggle with someone who has already dealt with that same issue?

There are divine opportunities out there awaiting your engagement as either the provider or recipient of support. But it takes a keen awareness, emotional and spiritual sensitivity, and an act of risk taking to recognize and respond to these opportunities.

Recently, I was talking about divine optimal matches in an interpersonal communication course, and I had the students write down a couple of their own life struggles or pain points. Then I had them get into groups of three and (if they felt comfortable doing so) share these struggles and discuss how God might use them as the provider or recipient of support in one of these areas. After a short period of small group discussion, I asked if any of the groups would be comfortable sharing what they discussed. This one group of three young women raised their hands and shared that in that moment they realized that each one of them came from a home that had an alcoholic father. They didn't know that about one another before, and if they hadn't taken the opportunity to open up and share, they probably would have never realized that common source of pain. From that point on in the semester those three young women were inseparable.

You can easily recognize when someone comforts you in the way that they themselves have received comfort from God. You experience a new type of listening, empathy, and wisdom-filled advice that others don't bring to the table. And, as a result, those people become unforgettable; you will never forget the way that person made you feel during that time of pain in your life. It's as if they were your own personal angel who arrived on the scene when you needed them most.

The Silver Lining of Our Personal Pain

When people engage in these conversations of divine optimal matching where they are able to provide comfort to another person from a place of past personal pain, they often report finding a silver lining to their past struggles. In fact, these people often discover a previously unknown purpose behind the negative experience—they even rebuild a sense of control in their lives and bolster their self-worth.[65] Ultimately, these divine optimal matches aren't just for the sake of the recipient of support, but there is also tremendous benefit to the provider of support. This actually brings an entirely new meaning to the 2 Corinthians 1:3–4 passage.

When I first applied these verses to this divine opportunity theme, I was really just doing so with the intent of highlighting the benefit to the recipients of support. It wasn't until now that I realized the full brilliance of these verses. By providing such comfort from our past pain we are gaining empowerment, control, and purpose over those past circumstances. Jesus's reminder that it is more blessed to give than to receive shines through even in the act of comforting from a place of past pain. It can be more of a blessing to provide comfort than to receive it. I bet if we had a chance to sit down and talk with Wendy, she would share with us how blessed she was to be able to comfort Elissa, and how by doing so she found her own sense of purpose, control, and self-worth.

In Elissa's story she even raises the question, "What if Wendy would have said, 'No, I'm sorry, I'm really busy, I can't talk to you right now'? Or what if she had said, 'That's kind of an embarrassing subject for me, I don't like to talk about my kid and his special needs, I want others to think my family is perfect'?" If Wendy would have told Elissa no in an attempt to avoid any potential embarrassment or in an attempt to hide her family's struggles, she would have deprived Elissa of this life-altering comfort. Not only that, but Wendy would have also deprived herself of gaining a sense of purpose and control around her own past struggles. I have no doubt that God rewards those who take the vulnerability risk of comforting from a place of past pain.

Consider it from this perspective. In another recent interpersonal communication class, I brought in guest speakers from the counseling center to talk to the students about suicide prevention and depression. More specifically, we discussed how to approach people with depression and suicidal

thoughts from an interpersonal perspective. This raised some great awareness and discussion. After the class was over, one of the students, Joy, came
up to me and said that her family has had several direct experiences with
suicide. She had known an alarming number of family members and family
friends who had committed suicide. I asked her if she would be willing to
share her experiences with the other students in the following class period.
Joy agreed and prepared some comments.

The next class period, Joy came in and shared her personal connections
to suicide, depression, and how serious this topic will be at some point in
each of their lives. Through her personal stories, she reminded the students
of their need to be emotionally sensitive and prepared so that they can
handle delicate conversations when they arise with others. After the class
ended, one of the other students caught Joy before she headed out. He
opened up with her about his own struggles with depression and suicidal
thoughts. He told her how important it was that she took that opportunity
to open up, then he thanked her for having the courage to share and how
much that meant to him.

By allowing herself to be vulnerable and available to this opportunity,
Joy was able to provide awareness to some and comfort to others. Who
knows, maybe this was the first time that young man had shared his depression with a friend. It could have been a breath of fresh air when he
needed it most. Beyond that, as Joy shared with me about her conversation
with that fellow student, I could see it in her face how much she was also
personally rewarded by the experience.

Below is another divine opportunity that highlights God's divine optimal matching. Again, God repurposes the pain from one person's past to
the benefit of another in the present. This story is from Karley, a twenty-
one-year-old college student and employee at In-N-Out Burger.

> To start, I need to give you a little background and context to
> set up some of the significant aspects that led to my divine op-
> portunity, because it took place a couple weeks ago at In-N-Out
> Burger where I work.
>
> One of the first signs in this buildup to the divine opportunity
> is that right when I got to work, my manager came up and told
> me that I was going to be outside taking orders. I hadn't been
> outside to take orders since my promotion almost six months
> before. Initially, I wasn't looking forward to it; I thought this was
> a thing of the past for me. It's quite boring outside. All you're
> doing is taking orders the entire shift and occasionally checking

the trashcans. If I'm being completely honest, I was thinking, "Oh, I really don't want to be outside."

The second thing that happened is that right before I was getting ready to head outside it began to rain. Now I was like, "Okay, I really don't want to do this." But my manager told me that he was going to send someone else out with me to hold an umbrella so I didn't get wet. So now, it was California cold, rainy, and I was heading out to do a job that I thought I was promoted past. By the way, I have worked for In-N-Out for five years and I have never seen them send two people out in the rain to where one person's sole job was to just hold an umbrella.

But we headed outside with the umbrella to take orders. Because it was raining, we weren't too busy. Honestly, when it's not that busy, there's no need to even be outside because we can just take all the orders from inside through the intercom. I was wondering, "Why are we even out here? This is just really unexpected and unnecessary."

Then one man pulled up. He was about fifty years old, wearing glasses, and he had a Chocolate Lab in the back seat. Whenever, customers come with dogs in their car I always end up talking more to the dogs than I do to the people. I just really love dogs. I have three dogs of my own—one Chocolate Lab and two little Maltipoos (half Maltese, half Toy Poodle).

Whenever people have a dog with them I already feel a connection that I don't have with others. If a person has a dog in their car, you can tell that they love them a lot, because typically people don't let their dogs ride in their cars unless they have a special relationship with them. When he pulled up I said, "Hi," and then immediately started talking to the dog, "Hi, what's your name?" He said, "Oh, this is Abby." I said, "Hi, Abby, how are you?" He said, "Oh, well, we're not that good." So I said, "What's wrong?" He said, "We had to put Abby's brother down a couple of days ago. Her brother was another Chocolate Lab, so we've been pretty distraught over the last few days."

I told you that I have a Chocolate Lab, but I also used to have a Yellow Lab that we had to put down exactly a year ago. The same thing happened to my Chocolate Lab when we had to put the Yellow Lab down. He was a mess. Right after the loss, the Chocolate Lab started to howl, and I had never seen him howl before that happened. It was like he was crying.

So right when he said that he had just put down the other dog, I knew exactly what he was feeling and going through. It's heartbreaking to see your dog being such a mess and not being able to do anything about it. I told the guy, "I'm so sorry. That exact same thing happened to my family a year ago." He said, "Oh, I just didn't know what to do, so I got a new puppy and now that puppy has contracted Parvo." Parvo is one of the worst diseases a puppy can get, causing vomiting and diarrhea to the point of severe dehydration. Almost all of them die from it.

I was thinking, "No way, when we had to put our dog down, we also got a new puppy and our puppy also got Parvo." So I explained this to him that we had similar dogs, one that died, one that was a mess and howling, and a new puppy with Parvo. Our similarities were so crazy. I had never known anyone else with such a uniquely similar situation.

I got to tell him that when our Maltipoo got Parvo, it was only three pounds, and when the vet spayed our dog he actually pulled through and lived. Our puppy didn't have any more issues after that. I shared with him that since his puppy was a Lab and almost fifteen pounds, if the vet spayed him he would have a good chance of pulling through as well. I was really able to connect with him on an emotional level and also provide him with some hope, which, he seemed pretty hopeless over the situation to begin with.

Keep in mind, here we were having this full-blown conversation back and forth about our dogs, with all sorts of details, and there is no one else coming through the drive-thru. This is In-N-Out, which is *always* busy, and there are no other customers. We had this little window of time together to talk and connect.

Then I had this strong urge that I wanted to pray for him. Usually, I don't say that to anybody but family and friends. Plus, I'm at work, and I don't know what this man's religious views are or anything else about him. But I just felt like I really needed to tell him that I was going to be praying for him. So I just went for it and told him that I was going to be praying for him, Abby, and his puppy. He said, in a surprised toned, "Wow, you'd do that for me?"

Now a few cars started to come in, so I wasn't going to be able to pray for him right then and there, but I told him I would definitely be praying. With such seriousness, he said, "You don't know how much that means to me that you would pray for me." So I was thinking that maybe it was just this guy and his two dogs. He hasn't mentioned anyone else in his life other than these dogs. Perhaps he doesn't have a family or anyone close who would pray for him or care for him and his situation in a prayerful way. He said, "Thank you so much for being willing to do that for me."

Cars were starting to roll in, so I had to wrap it up with, "So you had a burger, fries, and drink, and that will be $5.78 at the window." Awkward, I know. But after my shift, I went home and I prayed for him and his dogs. In my heart I have this peace about him and his puppy. I know this may not be a very big deal for most people, but I could tell that these dogs really meant a lot to him. I felt like this was a special moment for the two of us. And although there were three of us, with the other employee standing there holding the umbrella, this was just a moment for the two of us. The other employee didn't catch the importance of this at all. Afterward, all he said was, "You love dogs way too much." I guess some people just won't get what this moment was all about.

That closing statement from Karley has truth to it. When it comes to divine opportunities, oftentimes those who are not directly involved have no idea what is going on. In fact, often they will be downright skeptical and sarcastic about what you may have said and done for someone else. These moments are particularly powerful for the comforter and comforted; the bystanders won't always recognize what they just witnessed. In fact, by trying to include an emotionally and spiritually disengaged bystander you could be inviting unnecessary distractions into the moment.

Bonus Divine Intervention (You're Welcome)

Below is a bonus divine intervention that further illustrates this point that when God seeks people out for a divine opportunity, He occasionally tunes others out to avoid them interfering in a powerful moment.

Our family loved to go to Stone Harbor, New Jersey, for vacation. As my kids grew up they loved to go there. On this particular trip they were grown, and so we decided to go to the shore and reminisce about all the experiences at Stone Harbor.

You first have to understand something. My wife is a book reader, and when she is reading a book I am not in her mind at all. And when we go to the beach, she likes to get a big book and sit and read. So this day at the beach, I really wanted her attention. But she was in a sand chair under an umbrella reading a book. Then I saw a little boy making a sand castle and so I decided to get down on all fours and draw a heart in the sand that says david loves becky. I didn't draw a small heart either; it was a big heart. I'm an older man, down on all fours, digging in the sand along with all these little kids.

I had some attention—all but my wife's attention. So I was in the sand and I wrote david loves becky, and I waited. I stood back and she turned the page, so I thought, "I've got to make it fancy to attract her." I went down to the beach to get seashells, multi-colored seashells, and I was going to line the outside of the heart with seashells and hope that maybe that would get her attention. At this point, everyone around was wondering what I'm doing except for her. I came back with an armload of sea-shells, I dropped the seashells and made a racket, and she turned the page.

I took the seashells and I outlined the heart and she didn't do anything, so I said to her, "Becky, do you notice anything differ-ent?" And here's what she did: she put the book down and she said to me, "Oh, that's very nice." Then she looked at her watch and said, "I better go make dinner." Then she got up with her book and walked to the house we rented, leaving the umbrella and the beach chairs for me to return. Well, I was not feeling very good right then. It was not going as planned. So I decided that I was not going to let this destroy our family time. I got the umbrella and beach chairs and told the kids that we've had to go and I just forgot about it. I left behind the heart in the sand, and the fancy seashells, and the david loves becky still written in the sand.

Part of the tradition that I have is to get up early and enjoy the beach with a cup of coffee and a newspaper. So the next morning I went to the donut place to get a cup of coffee. I was in line because everyone else on the beach kind of has the same deal, where they want to get a coffee and get out on the beach and soak in the beautiful ocean.

I was standing in line when the couple in front of me looked back, and then they turned back around and started talking to each other again. I could tell that they were talking about me. Of course, I looked myself over to make sure that I looked all right. Sure enough I was okay, but I was wondering what they're talking about. Then the man turned around and said to me, "Were you on the beach yesterday?" I said, "Yes." He said, "Did you by any chance draw a heart in the sand?" I said, "Yeah." And she turned around and said, "Go ahead and tell him." I replied,

"Tell me what?"

He said to me, "My wife and I started out our marriage in a beautiful relationship, and then we had children, and complications, and our jobs brought extra pressures. Well, we grew apart to the point that we were talking about divorce. And my wife said to me, 'Why don't we go to Stone Harbor, where we've gone many times, and why don't we try one last time to make this marriage work.'" She said, "Yesterday we were on the sand for the final full day, and today is the day that we are going home." They were just getting a cup of coffee and about to head out to go home.

She said, "This whole week has been horrible, nothing has gone right, and we have fought all week long, and we thought we were sure that we would get a divorce. The only problem was how we would navigate this with the kids. So yesterday was the last day on the beach, but we saw you doing something in the sand that puzzled us. So after you left, we both got up from our sand chairs to see what you did. We both stood there over this huge heart that says david loves becky.

And he said to me, "My name is David and her name is Becky! And when I saw that heart, something happened in me. I realized what I had, and I turned to Becky and said, 'I do love you.' And standing there, God did something in our lives beyond explanation."

God is faithful. Their relationship was dissolving, but there was a moment on the beach. And you want to hear the rest of the story? I know now why my wife wasn't taken with the heart—it's because it wasn't for her. It was for two umbrellas down, where children weren't going to have a mom and dad under the same roof anymore, where a husband and wife were going to say goodbye. Two umbrellas down, God saw them and His faithfulness lives on. David loves Becky.

God can intervene in people's lives however He sees fit. I believe He desires to use us, to do so, far more regularly than we will ever realize. I beg you to take time to prayerfully consider how God might use you to comfort others. It's not just to the benefit of others, but it's to the great benefit of your own personal growth. Don't rob yourself of the experience of being used by God. If you make yourself available and you're willing to interact with your own vulnerabilities, God will gift you with your own firsthand experiences of divine opportunities and a mounting manna jar of stories of God's blessings to share with the next generation.

Discussion Questions

1. How have you experienced God's divine optimal matching? Has God repurposed a painful experience from your past to minister to someone else's pain in the present? Or vice versa?

2. What are a few of the painful experiences from your past that God may call you to share in order to bring comfort to others in the present?

3. Review Elissa's story one more time, and closely consider her closing comments in the final three paragraphs. Who is someone in your life that you have been turning down and saying no to their particular request? Is it time to say yes, and let God move you in a new direction?

Chapter 11

Some Plant, Some Water, but God Makes Things Grow

The Lord has assigned to each his task. I planted the seed, Apollos watered it, but God made it grow. So neither he who plants nor he who waters is anything, but only God, who makes things grow. The man who plants and the man who waters have one purpose, and each will be rewarded according to his own labor. For we are God's fellow workers; you are God's field, God's building.

—1 Corinthians 3:5–9

This may be the single most important chapter of the book, with the single most important message about divine opportunities. The message is this: divine opportunities are more than just the monumental moments in ministry, and they are more than just the life-saving moments of bringing someone to faith. They include *every* moment from the smallest act of planting a seed of hope, encouragement, and support to the life-altering moments when God transforms a life and someone accepts Christ for the first time.

My greatest fear in writing this book is that including such transformational divine opportunity stories with miraculous outcomes will lead you to think that those are the only kind of divine opportunities, or that those are the only kind that matter, which couldn't be further from the truth. The simple reason for including such awe-inspiring divine opportunities throughout the book is simply for marketing purposes. Let's be honest, if I didn't include such big divine opportunities, you probably wouldn't have read this far in the book.

The fact of the matter is that when we need inspiration we don't go to the basics; we go to the "best." Think about the All-Star Weekend for Major League Baseball (MLB). They spend an entire evening celebrating the Home Run Derby, *not* the Single to Left Derby. The MLB spends a lot of time and effort to get people excited to watch players regularly crush the ball 450 plus feet out of the park, rather than players who regularly hit a blooper into left field for a single. When my friends and I needed to get psyched for a soccer game in high school, we would watch a video called *101 Greatest Goals*, *not* 101 Greatest Throw-Ins, and *not* 101 Greatest Thigh-Traps.

Society spends a lot of time and energy celebrating the best and brightest moments in life. This chapter is dedicated to reminding us to celebrate both the small steps and the big leaps in conversation. There is a great TED Talk entitled "Everyday Leadership" by Drew Dudley, which is a wonderful example of how small moments can make a big difference. Granted, Dudley isn't talking in Christian terms or even spiritual terms, but he makes the following point about leadership that translates perfectly for divine opportunities. Dudley says:

> I worry sometimes that we spend so much time celebrating amazing things that hardly anybody can do that we've convinced ourselves that those are the only things worth celebrating, and we start to devalue the things that we can do every day, and we start to take moments where we truly are a leader and we don't let ourselves take credit for it, and we don't let ourselves feel good about it.... As long as we make leadership something bigger than us, as long as we keep leadership as something beyond us, as long as we make it about changing the world, we give ourselves an excuse not to expect it every day from ourselves and from each other.

I'd like to do a hybrid of quoting and paraphrasing Dudley here to translate this into divine opportunity terms and continue this thought. We've made divine opportunities into something that is only for the spiritually gifted, we've made divine opportunities into something that is beyond our abilities as an everyday Christians, we've made divine opportunities about monumental changes, and we've taken the title of divine opportunities, and we have treated it as if it's something that one day we're going to deserve to participate in. But to allow ourselves to think that we could be regularly engaging in divine opportunities right now means a level of responsibility and religious preparedness that we're not comfortable with.

The point is that no single divine opportunity is any better than any other because each divine opportunity, big or small, is needed all the same. And no Christian is any better than any other because it simply comes down to those who give themselves versus those who withhold themselves.

To illustrate this point, I want to take a close look at 1 Corinthians 3:6–9, which draws out this idea that ministry is about planting seeds, watering, and allowing God to make things grow. These verses remind us that the Lord has assigned each their task for a particular purpose, and no task, purpose, or person is greater than any other. Most importantly, regardless of the task, big or small, we are God's fellow workers—and what an honor and privilege it is to be a fellow worker of the Creator of the universe. There is no higher calling than that.

Starter, Reliever, and Closer

I want you to think about divine opportunities from the perspective of pitchers on a baseball team. Each baseball team is made up a whole host of pitchers. The majority of pitchers fall into one of three categories—starters, relievers, and closers. The starters specialize in opening games up and pitching as far into the game as possible. The whole idea is that these pitchers will get the team off to a strong start so that others can take it the rest of the way. The relievers specialize in entering games midstream. Their goal is to pick up where the starter left off and provide support in the middle of the game. Then there are the closers who specialize in coming in at the end of the game to close it out strong. The closers finish out the last couple of innings and bring it home in the end.

I noticed a similar pattern in the stories people shared with me about divine opportunities. When it comes to divine opportunities, God uses us in a variety of roles. Sometimes God uses us as the starter, as we go out and plant seeds of hope in people's lives. At other times God uses us as the relievers, as we take over for the starters in relationship with others and we continue the encouragement and support where the starters left off. And in some cases God uses us as the closers, where we pick up after the starters and relievers, and are a part of the growth.

This is an empowering way to view your role in divine opportunities. Think about the role that God tends to use you the most—starter, reliever, or closer? For me personally, I would say that God uses me the most often as the starter or reliever. My personal strength is in planting and watering seeds. My stories involve smaller moments of blessings through encouragement, support, and hope. However, my father-in-law, David, has been blessed to be the closer on several occasions where God sends him in at the end and seals the deal with people who are on the fence about their faith in Christ.

But the point I want to make sure you do *not* miss is that no role—starter, reliever, or closer—is any more important than the other. For example, David's stories of God using him as the closer would not have been possible if other starters and relievers had not been obedient and faithful in ministering to that person through encouragement, support, and setting a good example of Christ's love prior to that transformational moment.

It is easy for starters and relievers to grow frustrated by divine opportunities as they convince themselves that they don't have any stories of their own. I would like to argue that it isn't that the starters and relievers don't have stories of divine opportunities, but rather people in those roles don't often hear "the rest of the story" in order to realize the significant role they played in God's plan. I can relate with people who listen to stories like David's and think, "What I would give for one of those stories." The benefit of being used as a closer is that these people are often present for the moment of growth, so they are made aware of the divine opportunity that has taken place. The starters and relievers aren't as regularly made aware of how important and vital their conversational act of obedience was in the ongoing journey for that person.

This is why the moment I look forward to the most is when I get to heaven and God reveals to me "the rest of the story" that occurred after all my small acts of encouragement and support in people's lives. What a fun and glorious moment that will be. I am right there with you if you are one of those people who have been planting and watering seeds without ever getting to see or hear "the rest of the story." If you don't approach this with the right attitude and frame of mind, then it can be incredibly frustrating and demoralizing. After all, this is the equivalent of only being allowed to watch the first of half of every movie for your entire life, then, finally getting to heaven as the ending to every movie you ever watched is finally revealed to you. What a moment of sweet satisfaction that will be.

Before providing some illustrations to these points, I want to take a moment to warn you of one particular fallout from this starter, reliever, and closer analogy. It is simply this: we can each risk limiting ourselves to the role of starter and reliever by sticking to our social comfort zone. I want to acknowledge that while we do a vast majority of starting and relieving, it would be a shame to deprive yourself of being a closer when God calls you to step up be a part of significant growth. Let God use you however He sees fit; don't limit yourself to one role or another. Be prepared to enter another's life whenever, wherever, and however God desires.

Below are three divine opportunity stories that illustrate how God has used particular people at certain times in each of the three roles. I pray that this is a reminder to you that no person, no role, and no divine task is greater than any other. For God assigns each their task, for a particular purpose, and He rewards each of His fellow workers according to their labor.

Some Plant—Starter

This first divine opportunity comes from Jeremy, whose story is a great example of how God uses us to plant seeds in the lives of others.

> A few years back, I was living in Minneapolis, Minnesota. At the time, I was working as both a rock climbing instructor at a facility in town, as well as a youth pastor at a local church. The rock climbing was more of an interest, hobby, and paycheck; pastoring was my ultimate passion and career goal.
>
> Around the time of this divine opportunity, I had been working for the rock climbing facility for about four years. I had developed some really great relationships with other instructors there. There was one guy, Nick, whom I worked with. For the first two years of working with him I would occasionally notice that he would have a bit of an odd attitude toward me. It was never negative, but when faith topics came up he was a little touchy. I always felt like I was walking on ice with him, because he knew I was a Christian youth pastor. But after two years of working with him I found out that he was gay. When I realized that I was able to make much more sense out of his previous reactions.

Nick and I worked together for two years, then he moved away for a year, and then he came back and we worked together for one more year. While he was away, my wife and I got pregnant—mostly she was pregnant and I was just supporting. But by the time Nick returned, my wife was nine months pregnant. Toward the end of the pregnancy, my wife began to feel like something wasn't quite right; she hadn't felt the baby kick in a little while. She got nervous and rushed to the hospital. It was then that the doctors gave us some of the most heartbreaking news we've ever received. They told us that our baby boy had developed a tight knot in the umbilical cord which cut off the necessary life nutrients, and he had died. At nearly full-term, my wife had to deliver and we had to bury our baby boy. It was the most difficult and lowest point in our lives, and Nick witnessed me go through this time during our final year of working together.

It was about eight months into this grieving when both Nick and I were quitting our jobs at the rock climbing facility. We were quitting on the exact same day; we even shared a goodbye party together with the rest of the staff. On the final day of work, I was scheduled for the morning shift and Nick was scheduled for the evening shift. Really, we shouldn't have crossed paths at all, because his shift didn't start until two hours after mine ended. However, as my shift came to a close I was packing up all my stuff in the break room, and in walked Nick. We sort of chitchatted for a bit, hugged, and said goodbye. I had my hand on the door handle when he said to me, "Can I ask you a question?" I said, "Of course." Then Nick asked, "How did you deal with the death of your son?"

This question sort of took me back a bit, not because this topic was off limits but it did come a bit out of nowhere. Nick's question sort of piqued my interest as to why he was asking and why he was asking at that particular time. I took a quick breath, and I asked, "What do you mean?" Nick said, "I've just been going through some stuff lately and I'm just trying to piece it together and figure it out." I replied, "Well, you know that I'm a Christian, so for me I've really made it through this time because I have God Himself and His Son Jesus Christ to lean on." I shared with him Psalm 23. I said, "This is the passage that I hold very dear, because I felt like this was my journey after losing my son—walking through the valley of the shadow of death."

This immediately opened a door for us to talk about faith and what he believed, and so we sat in the break room for an hour, completely uninterrupted, as we had this heart-to-heart about surviving in the midst of life's chaos. Finally, it reached a point where I just asked him, "What is it exactly that you are dealing with, Nick?" He turned to me and said, "You know my boyfriend and I have been dating for about a year?" I said, "Yeah." Nick continued, "Well, we just broke up three days ago." I looked at him and said, "Man, that must be really hard, that's really painful."

Nick got a puzzled looked on his face, somewhat shocked at what I had said and that I would care about the pain that he would feel from his homosexual relationship that I didn't agree with. I could tell he had somewhat of a stereotypical view of Christians, so I think my empathizing toward his lost relationship was a bit of a surprise at first. Then he said, "Yeah, it is really hard and I am struggling to make sense of it all." I said, "When relationships end they can be about the worst feeling in the world, kind of like somebody dying. In fact, it's like a death, a death of a relationship." Nick said, "Yeah, that's how I feel."

Truly, I felt honored and privileged that he would open that door of his life to me. From there, I was just trying to be sensitive to what God wanted me to do in that moment. I whispered a desperate prayer to Jesus to help me say the right words. I did my best to help Nick process through his emotions by talking about them and sharing them openly. I simply comforted him in the moment as a friend, because I genuinely cared about him. Ultimately, though, I felt like this was a God-ordained moment and this was Nick's chance to hear from God.

I think the death of my son—while even at this point, I still have problems saying God used it, as if God is uncaring. In fact, when my son died people would say, God's going to use this. I wanted to slug them right in the teeth because to me, in that moment of pain, I didn't want to hear that. As much as it's true, in some respect, that if you yield your pain to God, He will make something beautiful out of something tragic. But these people made it sound like God was some sort of scrap picker, that God was just grabbing things out of my life so that He could use it for His own uncaring use. I'll say it this way: in that moment all the pain that I had gone through was suddenly useful to somebody else, to bring them through their own pain. So while God didn't cause the death of my son, He did repurpose it and gave it some perspective other than just pain. I am able to look back and say,

"Somebody's life was made better because I was able to identify with their pain."

Before we said goodbye, I asked him, "Nick, you've shared some of your beliefs with me, do you mind if I share some of mine with you?" I said, "I think God's personal and He loves us and He responds to prayer." Then I asked him, "Can I pray for you and with you, over your situation and your move?" He said, "Sure." So I stood next to him and put my hand on his shoulder and just prayed a short prayer. I don't think it was anything earth shattering or eloquent, it was just a simple blessing. I asked God to bless his life as he sought the truth, that He would reveal Himself to him, and that He would help him through his pain. Then we embraced again and said goodbye.

There was no altar call and no big response. However, about a week later I got a Facebook message from Jen, a mutual friend of ours. Jen was a former coworker who was also a Christian. Nick happen to visit her in Colorado on his move to Utah. Jen sent me a Facebook message saying, "Jeremy, I don't know what you said to Nick the other night when you talked to him, but thank you for being a great witness of Jesus's love to him when he most needed it. Nick and I had some incredible conversation tonight at dinner about Christianity. I was curious why all the sudden he was asking me about my faith, and he referenced his conversation with you. So let me say thank you for being kind and sensitive to him in that moment."

What I love about Jeremy's story is that we get to see both aspects of planting and watering a seed in a single illustration. Here God used Jeremy to a plant a seed in Nick's life, which is then watered by Jen in Colorado, as shared in her Facebook message. Jeremy, the starter in this sense, certainly gave Nick something to think about in terms of dealing with life's disappointments and setbacks. Then Jen, the reliever, got an opportunity to continue the conversation and water the seed that Jeremy had planted a week earlier. Without Jeremy's initial divine opportunity, Nick would not have likely raised the topic of Christianity with Jen a week later. Both Jeremy and Jen's roles are equally important, as will be the interactions of all those people who continue to water the seed planted in Nick. I'm sure there will be Christians who move him forward as well as backward along his journey.

Some Water—Reliever

The second divine opportunity comes from John, who provides us with a great illustration of what it means to water—support, encourage, and nurture—the spiritual development of others.

A couple weeks back I was at Target with my wife and two boys. We were walking around picking up a few items when the boys headed off in one direction with their mom and I headed off in a separate direction to look for some shoes. On my way to the shoe section, I looked down one of the aisles to my left and saw a man who attends our church. So I went over to this guy and said hello. We greeted each other and started a conversation. However, I thought this was just going to be the typical back and forth banter and then I would be on to my shoe hunt.

As we were talking, though, I could tell that something was really bothering him, something was on his mind that he wasn't sharing. As we continued to talk, I asked, "What brings you here?" Well, obviously he was buying something, right? (He had a CD in his hand.) But I asked him the question as more of a probe than really needing to know what exactly he was buying. I felt like there was something going on in this conversation that wasn't being expressed, and there was something about the conversation that went beyond words. I asked him the question, "What brings you here?" to see if he was ready to share what was really going on. If not, that was fine, but if so, we would go from there.

It started off as a general reply about being in the music aisle, but then I could see his nonverbals shift, he got a bit more emotional, and then he said, "Well, I'm waiting to meet my ex-wife to talk about our daughter going to college in another state and all the ramifications of that." He continued, "I'm not looking forward to this conversation because there's a lot of tension in our lives, and there always has been since before the divorce. There's a lot of conflict, and she has been very mean and ugly and condescending in our relationship."

He was feeling a lot of anxiety; he really didn't want to have this conversation and risk it all blowing up in his face. He just wanted to deal with the facts and move forward. He approached it and thought, "Well, I have to do this because this is best for my daughter." He went on to share a bit more with me about their story, tension, and pain. As he did, he was emotional and it became clear to me that this was a divine opportunity.

The Lord brought my family to Target, then I happened to go one way and my wife and children happened to go another. After all, this conversation probably wouldn't have progressed past the cordial greetings if the whole family were around. To be honest, I was actually a little bit lost as I was trying to find where the sneakers were located. Also, I'm a pretty fast-paced kind of guy, and while I'm friendly I normally would have said "hey" and kept going. I was on a mission and we didn't have a lot time. Ultimately, I just felt impressed to stop and go over and greet him and start a conversation. Of course, I anticipated a very brief conversation.

There was a lot going on here so I began to ask questions and he began to open up. I interjected some thoughts here and there, but predominately I just listened. He told me what was happening and that the pain and anxiety was coming from the nerves of his daughter moving far away for college, the burden of costs involved, and the tension in the relationship between his ex-wife and current wife. Not to mention this conversation was now just a few minutes away.

After he shared a few more details, I responded, not with advice, but more affirmation and encouragement. As he started to speak, it was in that moment I knew that I was there as a divine opportunity to be an instrument of God to bring grace, hope, and wisdom. I gave him one or two biblical principles that I thought may help him navigate the emotions of the moment. Then I said, "Can we pray together?" So we began to pray right there in the music aisle of Target. It was just the two of us in the aisle when we prayed. He was emotional, and rightfully so, given the weight of the situation he was going to step into.

When we finished praying he was extremely grateful. He thanked me and expressed, "I can't believe that you came and we met at this very moment when I needed this reminder that God is with me." While he was grateful for me to be there for that support and encouragement, it wasn't about me. It was about God reminding him, through my presence, that God is with him and that God would help him.

He said, "You know, there are times when I'm just living out this faith in Christ as a follower, and sometimes I just know God loves me and He is with me. Other times I'm just wondering where He is because things don't always go well in this relationship." He said, "But time and time again God always shows Himself faithful, He always does something to confirm, always does something to encourage me and remind me, maybe offer me a word of wisdom." He continued, "I needed this moment before I went in there, and again, God reminded me and He brought you. What can I say, but that God is faithful." And that's kind of how we ended it. He went to have his conversation at Panera, and I went to find shoes.

A couple of days later I received an e-mail from him. The e-mail was an expression of thanks for the conversation, and a reiteration of a God moment. He was so grateful and it was a report. The conversation between him and his ex-wife went extremely well, better than almost all of their previous conversations. They really were able to talk through a good strategic plan of action, practically and financially, for their daughter and what that would look like so that they could communicate with one another in their daughter's best interest.

For him, this whole experience was a reminder that God was with him. He walked away from a prayer that was answered. He walked away from a fractured relationship that, even if it was a small step, moved toward healing not more brokenness. He walked away from the situation with hope that he and his ex-wife could be in a position to help their girl. And I think he walked away from the situation recognizing the value of the community of faith, and friendship, reminding him that he's not alone on this journey.

John's final statement really sums up the role of watering and acting as the reliever. It's all about showing others the value of the community of faith, friendship, and reminding others that they are not alone on their journey through life. Everyone is in constant need of watering; there isn't a single person on this planet who couldn't use regular encouragement and support. No one will ever reach a place in their life or in their faith where they no longer need people to come around them to be that form of relief, reprieve, and reconciliation. Even the lead pastor at your church, whom most would look to as the spiritual leader, could regularly use someone to come alongside them and support and encourage them and be their source of motivation.

God Makes Things Grow—Closer

The third divine opportunity comes from my father-in-law, David, who provides a wonderful account of what it means to be used by God in a moment of growth and increase in someone else's life. Here is the closer at it again.

It was the Sunday before Valentine's Day that I was at home looking over my message. It was around ten o'clock at night, right before I was going to go to bed, when the thought came to me to go out and buy a dozen roses. I was not wanting to go out and buy roses, so I was arguing with God that no store was open to buy roses. And the thought came to me, "Dillon's grocery store on Kearney." Dillon's grocery store had a twenty-four-hour flower section. So I decided that God was wanting me to do this, I didn't know why, but aggravated I went.

Aggravated. Now that's a key word—what God has to go through to bless people with divine opportunities. Not that we want to do it, but God loves people so much that He doesn't care how aggravated we get.

I got up, got presentable, and went to Dillon's grocery store. By the time I got to Dillon's grocery store all the roses were gone. That made me even more frustrated, because I had made a trip and I knew this was the day before Valentine's Day and there would be a run on the market.

This lady came up from the back and said, "Can I help you?" I said, "Well, I can see that you don't have any more roses, but I wanted to buy a dozen roses." She said, "Oh yes, we sold out hours ago of all of our roses." But another woman came up and said to her, "But there is a vase of a dozen roses in the back, so let me check." This other lady went back and brought out this beautiful presentation of a dozen roses—I mean it was an absolutely premium presentation. The note on it was that these people had reserved them, but they had called an hour ago and cancelled their order.

That's another important part of this story, because God had somebody order those roses and then cancel them so that they would be available. This way the roses wouldn't be put out to where other people could get them. They were being saved for somebody in the back.

The woman said, "You can buy these." So I got them hurriedly and paid for them. Then I went up to the church, and I put them on the organ speaker that is off to the side near the wall—it was a beautiful place to present them. I put the roses there, but completely forgot about them. Because they weren't in my order of worship, they weren't in my plans, they were very pretty, but I didn't see any purpose for them in my sermon.

As I was getting ready to preach my message the next day, I walked up to the pulpit, and out of the side of my eye I looked and saw the roses. I was frustrated because I wanted to use my time for preaching but I realized that there was something I needed to do. I got the roses and I explained to the congregation the story about how last night I had the thought to go and buy a dozen roses and how I went and bought them. I told them, "I would like to give these dozen roses to someone today."

I got the thought politically that I could honor Sister Wannenmacher, who is the former pastor's wife, with the roses. I went down off the platform and I was headed to Sister Wannenmacher to score some political points because everybody would love me honoring the former pastor's wife with these roses. But as I went down the platform the Holy Spirit put a thought in my mind, "Not on the left side, but on the right side. A visitor." I immediately turned from going up the left aisle, were Sister Wannenmacher was sitting, to the right aisle. I began walking not knowing who I was going to give them to, but I noticed a blonde-haired lady I had never seen before. I just assumed that she was a visitor.

Really, I wanted to get rid of them because they were taking up my preaching time. But I was reminded that God is concerned about people, He's not concerned about my preaching time or how political I can get. I walked up to this lady, and as I was approaching her, another thought came to me. The thought came to me, "Tell her that I love her and that I'm proud of her."

As I go up to her I said, "Ma'am, I just want you to know that God directed me last night to buy these roses, and as I was approaching you the thought came to me that God wanted me to tell you that He loves you and He's proud of you." And immediately, she broke down and began crying. But I wasn't really into her crying, because I want to get back to my sermon. I walked back to the pulpit, preached my message, I opened up the altar, and people came and responded to the message. Off to the side the blonde-haired woman was waiting patiently as I prayed for the people at the altar.

I went up to her and I said, "Can I help you?" She said, "You already have. Would you like to hear the rest of the story?" I said, "Yes!" She said, "I am a postal carrier. This week as I was delivering all the Valentines to people on my route, I just thought about my life, and how all my life I always wanted to please my dad. But my dad was one of those people who really didn't show love, and I wanted him to hug me and appreciate me. I was an athlete and I wanted him to go to my games and tell me that he loved me. So as I was delivering the mail, I stopped and I looked up to heaven and I said, 'If there is a God in heaven, I want You to tell me that You love me and that You're proud of me.' When you came up the aisle with those flowers, and you said those exact words—that God loves me and that He's proud of me—that was the answer to my prayer from God Himself. So before I go, I just wanted to tell you thank you for what you did for me this morning.

What David did was an act of obedience. What God did was answer a prayer in a miraculous fashion. I love what pastor and author Mark Batterson says: "Sometimes God shows up and sometimes God shows off." Here God was simply showing off. This was a divine opportunity story that will leave behind a wake of influence in others' lives as well. This is a story that will nourish the soul of others as they merely read it. I've read this story about fifty times and it gives my soul goose bumps every time. We recently spoke to Brenda, the woman mentioned in this story, and she said that even after all these years, that is still the most amazing and wonderful moment she has ever had. Brenda said that whenever she gets discouraged, she thinks back to that moment and it's like an anchor for her soul.

This is a reminder to those of you whom God has revealed to you "the rest of the story" to share those stories as often as you can. Share the stories in your manna jar with as many people as will listen, because each story has a lifetime of blessings that extend beyond the moment they occurred. Divine opportunities are the gifts that keep on giving.

68,000 Opportunities in a Lifetime

Here is one final thought from the social scientist part of me. Psychologists estimate that each person, on average, influences approximately 68,000 people in their lifetime. That includes all the people who cross your path throughout your lifetime from one-time interactions to those you know for more than thirty years. It includes small moments of influence as you spread your good or bad mood on to others, it includes the moments you influence someone as you order dessert after dinner, and it includes the moments you influence someone to grow deeper in their faith. So, based on the original estimate above, if I'm doing my math correctly (don't forget to carry the two, yep got it), that's at least 68,000 opportunities to let your light shine in the lives of others.

I realize that a big number like that can often seem a bit daunting and overwhelming, so don't forget that we are all part of a huge community of believers. As you influence each of those 68,000 people, you are merely playing a role—starter, reliever, or closer—on a team of believers that is being coached by God Himself. He calls us to be a light to the world and much of that is done through brief moments of support and encouragement to others in everyday conversation. If we are all obedient in our own small ways, each of those small acts of obedience will add up to one huge impact across our overlapping moments of influence.

Serve Who How—Screen-Saver Epiphany

A while back it dawned on me that despite how much time I spend researching, writing, and speaking about divine opportunities I am still quick to forget about the daily opportunities that I have to engage others. As I get busy and I rush around from one thing to the next, all that divine opportunity talk quickly goes straight out the window. In retaliation to such life distractions, I created a screen-saver for my phone so that anytime I tapped it, touched it, or turned it on, the first thing I would see are the words "Divine Appointment" across the screen. This was supposed to remind me that I needed to look up and look out and engage others and, perhaps, tap into more of those 68,000 waiting opportunities. But I seemed to struggle with that little visual reminder because when I focus too much on divine appointments, the end point, I tend to be thinking beyond something I can do and instead I'm waiting around for something God will do.

Recently, I started thinking that my little cell phone screen-saver trick might be more effective if it was a reminder of the small things I can immediately do rather than the big things God can do. What I needed was to figure out two things: (1) what exactly is my problem? and (2) what are the first steps to overcoming it? Well, my problems are ongoing, but this particular one boiled down to selfishness. When I get busy I get too focused on myself. As it turned out, I was spending entirely too much time living in Me-Town, USA. And I needed far more getaways from good ole Me-Ville. Brilliant insight, I know. When you have PhD you're able to think of amazing insights like the fact that selfishness causes you to turn away from others' needs and only focus on your own. You're welcome.

The second part of this was to figure out how to snap out of Me-Mode and dial into the lives of others. I had a recent epiphany of how to accomplish this the other day when I was watching a twelve-year-old clean dishes. Let me explain. We have some friends who will occasionally come over to our house for dinner, and every time they do their twelve-year-old, Halle, will do our dishes while we talk to her parents after dinner. That may not seem like the biggest deal to most, but my wife and I have a three-and-a-half-year-old and one-and-a-half-year-old, so doing our dishes is an enormous act of service. One less task to have to do at the end of our night is a breath of fresh air. Halle's service allows my wife and me to have long meaningful conversation with her parents while she frees us up of the mental and physical energy to do so.

This reminded me that I need to regularly ask myself, "Who is around me right now and how can I serve them?" The antidote to selfishness is service. The divine spark that I needed was the reminder that God calls us to serve others. In fact, He calls us to serve others is a wide variety of ways. Service is something that can be made small, while allowing God to make it big.

God can use acts of service that address tangible needs like washing dishes as well as acts of service that address intangible emotional needs as well. I can serve the person in front of me in line at the grocery store by simply saying, "Hi," asking their name, using their name in quick light-hearted conversation, and then saying, "Goodbye." Who knows what that brief dose of acknowledgement might have meant to them or how God might use that to segue into further conversation. Acts of service can be made as simple as words of encouragement, feelings of support, personal acknowledgement, and active listening.

Now, thanks to Halle, my screen-saver reads, "Serve Who How." That's my divine spark. Every time I look at my phone it's a reminder to serve someone right here, right now, in some small way. Who is around me, and how can I serve them? Is there someone I can introduce myself to and acknowledge as a person? Is there someone who needs a listening ear? Is there someone who needs a laugh? Is there someone who needs encouragement? Is there someone who needs a prayer? It's my job to pick out something small to do, and it's God's job to turn it into something big.

All this brings me to my final question: What kind of role are you going to play in the remainder of those 68,000 opportunities in your lifetime? The answer: "This little light of mine, I'm gonna let it shine, let it shine, let it shine, let it shine. Hide it behind an iPhone, no! I'm gonna let it shine. Hide it behind a frumpy-face, no! I'm gonna let it shine. Hide it behind a to-do list, no! I'm gonna let it shine, let it shine, let it shine, let it shine!"

Discussion Questions

1. Think of someone that has played each role in your own life—starter, reliever, closer. If you haven't already, let each of these people know how they impacted your life as a result of planting a seed, watering, or being used by God for the growth in your own personal journey. I might suggest a hand written letter, phone call, or face-to-face conversation with each of these people.

2. In which role (starter, reliever, or closer) do you feel God has used you the most? Which role do you feel the least confident or comfortable playing? In what ways do you feel challenged or intimidated by the role of the closer?

3. In what ways has this book expanded your view of divine opportunities?

Conclusion

A Prayer for Divine Opportunities

*Be very careful, then, how you live—not as unwise
but as wise, making the most of every opportunity, because the days are evil. Therefore do not be foolish, but
understand what the will of the Lord is.... Be filled
with the Spirit. Speak to one another with psalms,
hymns and spiritual songs. Sing and make music in
your heart to the Lord, always giving thanks to God
the Father for everything, in the name of our Lord
Jesus Christ. Submit to one another out of
reverence for Christ.*

—Ephesians 5:15–21

In the name of the Father, the Son, and the Holy Spirit. Dear heavenly Father, we come before You, as writer and reader, to pray for divine opportunities, Lord. Please God, awaken our souls to the opportunities that are all around us each and every day. Give us Your eyes and ears so that we can see the unseen and hear the unheard. Give us Your words as we step out in faith in conversation with others. Give us Your heart for others who cross our paths.

Please God, touch the heart of this reader in a new way that they have never experienced before. Inspire and motivate them to recognize opportunities that they would have previously walked right by. Give them a supernatural ability to catch the subtle movements of Your Spirit, and the will to stop and act on those promptings. Lord, let the imagery of "divine opportunities" be written in their heart, mind, and soul. Let the lifestyle of optimistic obedience be their calling from here on out.

God, we pray that You lead us *not* into temptation, but that You deliver us from evil. Don't let us be swept away in our own busyness and technology. Don't let us miss out on the opportunities that You are willing to grant us as relational gifts throughout our day. God, save us from the regret and guilt of missed opportunities. Call us out into a new way of living as we set our hearts and minds on the adventure of finding You in our conversations in the midst of everyday life.

Lord, we offer up to You all our fears, worries, and concerns. We ask that You replace those fears with confidence, self-assurance, and the kind of courage that comes from You and You alone. God, You are the only one who willingly accepts our worst and replaces it with Your best. We have no other place or person to go to that will gladly take up our fears, worries, and concerns and in exchange offer us confidence, courage, grace, and peace. Fill us with Your Spirit.

Lord, thank You for this reader. Thank You for this person who is uniquely and wonderfully made in Your image. You created him or her with a one-of-a-kind plan and adventure for their life. I pray that this reader has experienced You in and through this book, that they have encountered You through the stories contained in this book. I pray that You send this reader out to experience their own divine opportunity stories. God, lead them into their own firsthand experiences with You. We thank You for the secondhand experiences in this book, but we beg You to give us our own firsthand divine appointments. Give us life stories that we can add to our personal testimony of Your gracious love. Lord, please let our manna jars overflow with firsthand experiences that we may share with the next generation of believers.

God is good all the time. And all the time God is good. We pray for this in the name of Your Son and our Lord and Savior, Jesus Christ. And all God's people said, "Amen."

I Want to Hear the Rest of Your Story

I would love to hear about your divine appointments and missed opportunities. Please e-mail me at montague@divineopportunity. com to share the rest of your story. You can also visit www.divineopportunity.com to read more divine opportunities from other readers who have already shared their stories.

Appendix A

Relational Experiments

I have included two relational experiments that I have used in my interpersonal communication class. These experiments will force you to engage with others in a way that you wouldn't have otherwise. Some aspects of this might seem a bit awkward, forced, or uncomfortable. But I promise, if you are thoughtful and prayerful in your approach to these relational tasks, you will experience at least one breakthrough in a relationship that you wouldn't have had otherwise. I'm always amazed at the responses I receive from the students when they report back the results of these experiments.

There is a caveat though: you will get out of it what you put into it. You can expect results that match your effort. If you're halfhearted in your approach, you should expect lackluster outcomes. If you're wholehearted in your approach, however, you should expect something uniquely wonderful.

I know that many people don't like to force these kinds of conversations or interactions. Instead, they prefer to let these things happen "organically." Here's my question for those of you in that camp. How's that working for you? Is your organic approach to meaningful interaction happening on a regular basis? Do you have examples and stories of planting, watering, or growth? If you're not quite satisfied with the regular results, then perhaps it's time to be a bit more strategic in pursuing meaningful interaction. God can use strategically-orchestrated interaction just as well as He can naturally-arising conversation. As evidence of this, I have included an example of a student response from each experiment to show you what is possible.

Not-So-Random Acts of Kindness

The goal of this assignment is for you to perform five (different) *not-so-random acts of kindness* for family members, friends, roommates, classmates, or strangers. These are meant to be more outgoing, significant acts of kindness. I realize that all of you are likely performing many acts of kindness over the course of a week as it is. So these five acts of kindness need to take it to a whole new level. You may spread these out over the course of the week, but you do need to be intentional about preforming five specific acts of kindness that you would not have otherwise performed this week. These not-so-random acts of kindness should *not* be done through technology.

Here are some examples:

- Write a personal handwritten letter/note to someone who has been on your mind lately.
- Put together a care-package of someone's favorite treats, snacks, or trinkets.
- Drop off flowers for someone and attach a little note of encouragement.
- Treat someone to dinner at their favorite restaurant.
- Wash someone's car. (But don't use a rock to wash their car like my three-year-old son did for me. True story.)

Here are two examples I received from students who have done this for my class.

From Sara: "I thought it would be fun to drive to Santa Barbara for the weekend. This is my third year at APU and I have yet to go visit my grandparents who are in their eighties. It was out of the blue to visit; the only motive for me to drive there was this assignment and the realization that it had been a long time since I have seen my grandparents. It was crazy what happened. As I was driving to Santa Barbara, my mom called me to tell me that they discovered a tumor in my grandpa's liver. Driving, I was hit by emotions and thought to myself how amazing God's timing was. I spent the whole weekend with my grandparents, going out to dinner, shopping, and staying up late to watch TV with my grandpa. My grandpa, who already has Alzheimer's, looked at me after dinner on Saturday and said, 'Sara, I love when you come visit.' The trip was divine and it had an impact on the relationship I have with my grandparents. During a distressful time, I was able to distract them with my presence. Just a couple of days ago I was told that the tumor is actually cancerous. My mom told me that my grandma was explaining how thankful she was that I got to see my grandpa for what could have been one of my last times."

From Tiana: "I wanted to say thank you for encouraging us to send out a card to our parents. A little background: my mother passed away in 2007 from her battle with breast cancer. My grandmother, who is a widowed pastor's wife, has always held a prominent parenting role in my life, so I sent the card to her. My grandmother received the card today in the mail and called me, in tears, as I was leaving your class. She was truly touched by the card and was vulnerable with me in a way that she has never been before. I wanted to say thank you very much as it has motivated me to send more 'love letters' to my grandmother, and I want to encourage my siblings to do the same. Thank you for allowing us the time to reflect on it in class because I did not expect anything to come from it, but now I am able to build a deeper relationship with my grandmother in which I will cherish for a lifetime."

Low-Point Conversations

Ain't a soul on this entire earth that ain't got a burden to carry that he don't understand.

—from the movie The Legend of Bagger Vance

For this relational experiment, you should seek out three conversations. You can have these conversations with family members, friends, room-mates, classmates, or acquaintances. During each conversation, you will set out to have a meaningful conversation that allows you to better understand a low-point in each person's life (what, when, where, why, and how sorts of details), and how they were able to come out of the low-point (trying to identify strategies for working out of low-points in life). The strategies for recovery might include anything from prayer to conversations with people who were particularly supportive (friend, family member, or counselor). You will want to find out some details about the particular strategies that worked for them. If they said a supportive friend helped them through a tough time, find out why this person was particularly helpful, trustworthy, reliable, etc.

Pain funnel: You will accomplish all of this by navigating the conversa-tion using the questions in the pain funnel. If you veer off course from the questions in the pain funnel, that is certainly okay. The questions are just meant to be a helpful guide, helping people move from a broad perspective of curiosity to a more specific, narrowed, and detailed understanding. The pain funnel actually comes from a Sandler Sales Training orientation, but it works quite well in this circumstance as well. First, identify the low-point the person is willing to discuss with you, then start moving through the pain funnel.

Tell me more about that…

- Can you be more specific? Give me an example.
- How long has that been a problem?
- What have you tried to do about that?
- And did that work?
- How do you feel about that?
- Have you given up trying to deal with the problem?

There are four simple steps to follow for walking through these low-point conversations. Step one, set aside time for a personal conversation in a private setting with each of the three people. Step two, simply open up the conversation by asking, "Would you mind sharing with me a low-point that you have been through or are currently going through in your life?" Step three, be quiet and listen closely. Step four, start moving through the pain funnel.

Since the nature of these conversations is sensitive and confidential, I won't share any specifics from my students. However, as mentioned in the introduction to Part Three, I have come across just about every struggle you can imagine in the reading of the students' reports of their conversations. People have opened up and shared about abortions, miscarriages, deaths of parents/siblings/grandparents, physical abuse, sexual abuse, emotional abuse, bullying, and the list goes on and on. The things people have experienced in their past and the burdens that they carry around are heart wrenching.

These low-point conversations are not meant to reopen old emotional wounds. Instead, these conversations are meant to let people know that they are not alone, that they have people in their lives who care enough to take the time to sit, listen, empathize, and pray for them. These conversations are meant to be a reminder that everyone is dealing with some sort of low-point (no exceptions) and that there are plenty of opportunities out there just waiting for us to stop and pay a little bit of extra attention to them.

Here are some of the lessons my students have learned as a result of engaging in these conversations:

From A. J.: "This relational activity was eye-opening for me because it helped me see how difficult life can be even when everything appears positive on the surface. This activity has helped me think more critically about my judgments and responses to people. When you don't know the deeper hurt, it's easy to write off peoples' issues as character flaws. The truth is, people often carry around more hurt than I realize. I need to take the time to ask deep questions and truly listen. Although these were deep, serious conversations, I am excited to take this eye-opening learning with me into future conversations."

From Ashley: "What I gleaned from this activity was that everyone goes through tough times. It's so interesting to see how such relatively normal-looking unsuspecting people have these incredible feats they have overcome. It also makes me wonder who I might be interacting with everyday who could be facing some tough challenges I don't even know about. It makes me want to cut people a break, because I never know who might need a kind word or intentional smile. It makes me want to live intentionally and spread the good news of Christ because everyone needs Him everywhere all the time. I enjoyed this activity because it allowed people to open up about things that they wouldn't bring up unless specifically asked about it."

From Blakely: "I learned that people have struggles and burdens that we have no idea about. Even those close to us can have experiences that shaped them that we don't even know about. It's important to put the time and effort into connecting deeper with people and hearing their stories. One of the nicest things we can do for people is genuinely want to understand them."

From Jacova: "I deeply desire to see the people I love experience healing and see the truth about who they are in the midst of their pain and struggle. The most profound opportunities that I have had to speak these truths have occurred after I have taken a substantial amount of time to listen, inquire, and truly understand where my friend is coming from. I think people do not often get to share the depth of their experiences because their counterpart simply offers their opinion of the situation after hearing the upfront version of the story rather than digging into the heart of the issue. When we ask questions like 'Tell me more…' or 'Give me an example…" or 'How did that make you feel?' we allow space for true transparency and vulnerability."

Appendix B

Five TED Talks to Interpret in the Context of Divine Opportunities

None of these TED Talks are about divine appointments, yet each of them are about divine appointments. If you watch these videos with divine appointments in mind you will notice clear points of connection about emotional approachability, emotional availability, and emotional agility. These TED Talks have been very inspiring for me and my students when it comes to thinking about human interaction, social connection, and divine opportunity. I hope you find them engaging and helpful.

Connected, but Alone?
Sherry Turkle

Everyday Leadership
Drew Dudley

The Power of Vulnerability
Brene Brown

The Happy Secret to Better Work
Shawn Achor

Your Body Language Shapes Who You Are
Amy Cuddy

*You can search for these titles and speakers' names at www.ted.com to access the videos.

Acknowledgments

There are several people whom God has used to contribute to the fulfillment of this life calling.

David Watson, your divine appointment stories started it all. Your life experiences and passions sparked something inside of me that has now taken me on a remarkable journey through a PhD dissertation and now this book. I'm excited to see what God has in store for our continued journey ahead. Thank you for graciously allowing me to use your stories or as you would say, "God's stories." Those stories are a never-ending source of encouragement to all who hear or read them.

Jim Burns, you're ridiculously amazing! I have no idea why you took it upon yourself to help me, encourage me, and support me over the past four years, but I am *so grateful* that you have. You are the real deal. I've never met anyone who "talks the talk and walks the walk" like you do. I want to be Jim Burns when I grow up.

Tim Beals, thank you for taking a chance on me and on this book. Thank you for not giving up on this project and joining me on this journey through the ups and downs.

Loreen Olson, hard to believe this book started six years ago in your office when you approved my dissertation research topic. Whether you realized it or not, God was using you in a pivotal way—to provide an opportunity for people's divine appointment stories to be heard, shared, and transformed into practical lessons for us all. Thank you for your support as an advisor and a friend.

Thank you to all the participants who graciously shared your stories with me and have been willing to allow me to continue to use your stories over the years. Your stories and experiences have blessed my life in a way I can't even put into words. You inspire me and you will certainly continue to inspire others through the retelling of your amazing stories of observant and optimistic obedience to God's promptings.

Thank you to Canopy Church, C2 Church, and Bella Vista Assembly of God. You generously opened your doors to me for this project and your timely support was essential to completing this research. I pray that God continues to do a great work at each of your churches and for all who enter your doors.

Thank you to Azusa Pacific University for funding course releases so that I would have time to work on this project and see it through to completion. Thank you for remaining a God First higher education institution and giving us all (faculty, staff, and students) an opportunity to connect with Christ above all else.

Thank you to all my students at Azusa Pacific University over the past four years. Thank you for entertaining my talks, readings, and research on divine opportunities and missed opportunities. I greatly appreciate your support, encouragement, humor, and enthusiasm.

Thank you to all my friends and family in Missouri and Southern California, at Foothill Church and Redeemed Life Church. Thank you for your continued patience in our relationship, as I was ironically busy and disengaged as a result of writing this book, which is all about not being overly busy and seeking more engagement in relationships.

Endnotes

1   Putnam, R. D. (2000). Bowling Alone: The Collapse and Revival of American Community. NY: Simon & Schuster.

2   Serota, M. (2010, December 24). Happiness 101: Less tweeting, more meeting. The Christian Science Monitor. Retrieved from http://www.csmonitor.com.

3   Mehl, M. R., Vazire, S., Holleran, S. E., & Clark, C. S. (2010). Eavesdropping on happiness: Well-being is related to having less small talk and more substantive conversations. Psychological Science, 21, 539–541. doi:10.1177/0956797610362675.

4   Brittle, Z. (September 3, 2013). The digital age: A practitioner's perspective. The Gottman Relationship Blog. Retrieved from http://www.gottmanblog.com/digital-age/2014/10/30/the-digital-age-a-practitioners-perspective.

5   Buber, M. (1965). Dialogue (40). In Between Man and Man (R. G. Smith, Trans.). London: Routledge & Kegan Paul. (Original work published in 1947.)

6   Ibid. Additional Reading: Buber, M. (1958). I and Thou (2nd ed.; R. G. Smith, Trans.). New York: Charles Scribner's Sons. (Original work published in 1923.)

7   Buber, M. (1965). Dialogue (40). In Between Man and Man (R. G. Smith, Trans.). London: Routledge & Kegan Paul. (Original work was published in 1947.)

8   Heath, C., & Heath, D. (2010). Switch: How to Change Things When Change Is Hard. NY: Broadway Books.

9   Wiseman, R. (2010). The Luck Factor. Richmond, VA: Max Pitch Media.

10 Ibid.

11 Ibid.

12 Ibid.

13 Ibid.

14 This exercise is modified from a similar one that was originally done by Anthony Robbins (bestselling author and motivational speaker).

15 Hayashi, D. M. (2014). "When to trust your gut." In the Harvard Business Review: OnPoint, Emotional Intelligence: The Essential Ingredient to Success (80–87). Boston, MA: Harvard Business Review. (Original work published in 2001.)

16 Ibid.

17 Gottman, J.M. (2001). Preface. In The Relationship Cure: A 5 Step Guide to Strengthening Your Marriage, Family, and Friendships (xi). NY: Three Rivers Press.

18 Ibid.

19 Ibid., (65–87).

20 Ibid.

21 Buber, M. (1965). Dialogue (40). In Between Man and Man (R. G. Smith, Trans.). London: Routledge & Kegan Paul. (Original work published in 1947.)

22 Goleman, D. (2006). An instinct for altruism. In Social Intelligence: The Revolutionary New Science of Human Relationships (50–51). NY: Bantam Books. Study originally published by Darley, J. M., & Batson, C. D. (1973). "From Jerusalem to Jericho": A study of situational and dispositional variables in helping behavior. Journal of Personality and Social Psychology, 27(1), 100–108.

23 Ibid.

24 Pink, D. (2014). Crowd Control. TV show airing on the National Geographic Chanel.

25 Bradberry, T., & Greaves, J. (2009). Emotional Intelligence 2.0. San Diego, CA: TalentSmart.

26 Bradberry, T., & Greaves, J. (2009). Go on a 15-minute tour. In Emotional Intelligence 2.0 (156–157). San Diego, CA: TalentSmart.

27 Goleman, D. (2006). The emotional economy. In Social Intelligence: The Revolutionary New Science of Human Relationships (13–26). NY: Bantam Books.

28 American Psychiatric Association (2013). Other (or unknown) substance-related disorders. In Desk Reference to the Diagnostic Criteria from DSM-5 (277–279). Arlington, VA: American Psychiatric Association.

29 Serota, M. (2010, December 24). Happiness 101: Less tweeting, more meeting. The Christian Science Monitor. Retrieved from http://www.csmonitor.com.

30 Weingarten, G. (2007, April 8). Pearls before breakfast: Can one of the nation's greatest musicians cut through the fog of a D.C. rush hour? Let's find out. The Washington Post.

31 Ibid.

32 Gottman, J. M. (2015). As good as it gets. In Principia Amoris: The New Science of Love (170–176). NY: Routledge.

33 Ibid., (61–76).

34 David, S., & Congleton, C. (2014). Emotional agility. In the Harvard Business Review: OnPoint, Emotional Intelligence: The Essential Ingredient to Success (88–92). Boston, MA: Harvard Business Review. (Original work published in 2013.)

35 Goleman, D. (2006). You and It. In Social Intelligence: The Revolutionary New Science of Human Relationships (105–116). NY: Bantam Books.

36 The quote "loving regardless of results" came from a student in one of my interpersonal communication courses. However, I cannot recall which student said it or who they might have been quoting in the process.

37 Ekman, P. (2003). Conclusion: Living with emotion. In Emotions Revealed: Recognizing Faces and Feelings to Improve Communication and Emotional Life (231–236). NY: St. Martin's Press.

38 Ibid., (17–37).

39 David, S., & Congleton, C. (2014). Emotional agility. In the Harvard Business Review: OnPoint, Emotional Intelligence: The Essential Ingredient to Success (88–92). Boston, MA: Harvard Business Review. (Original work published in 2013.)

40 Ibid.

41 Ibid.

42 Ibid.

43 Ibid.

44 Ibid.

45 Ibid.

46 Burns, J. (2007). Confident Parenting. Minneapolis, MN: Bethany House.

47 Watson, David. Professor of Pastoral Ministries, North Central University. Personal communication. (September 2014.)

48 Shirran, M., Shirran, M., & Graham, F. (2012). Pause Button Therapy: Pause, Think, Decide, Act. Carlsbad, CA: Hay House.

49 Ibid.

50 Ibid.

51 Ibid.

52 Ibid.

53 Ibid.

54 Ibid.

55 Ibid.

56 Ibid.

57 The definition for "optimistic" was extracted from portions of the full definition listed on www.dictionary.com.

58 The definition for "obedience" was extracted from portions of the full definition listed on www.dictionary.com.

59 Hybels, B. (2006). Just Walk Across the Room: Simple Steps Pointing People to Faith. Grand Rapids, MI: Zondervan.

60 The One-Song Workout is referenced in Heath, C., & Heath, D. (2010). Switch: How to Change Things When Change Is Hard. NY: Broadway Books.

61 Carnegie, D. (1936). How to Win Friends and Influence People. NY: Simon & Schuster.

62 The Okay—Not Okay principle was originally proposed by Dr. Eric Berne in his book Games People Play: The Basic Handbook of Transactional Analysis. The principle was then expanded upon by Dr. Thomas Harris in his book I'm Okay—You're Okay. And it has even been used in sales programs by David Sandler. The version of the principle presented in this chapter is an abbreviated description.

63 Cutrona, C. E., & Russell, D. W. (1990). Type of social support and specific stress: Toward a theory of optimal matching. In I. G. Sarason, B. R. Sarason, & G. R. Pierce (Eds.), Social Support: An Interactional View (319–366). NY: Wiley.

64 Rook, K. S. (1987). Reciprocity of social exchange and social satisfaction among older women. Journal of Personality and Social Psychology, 52, 145–154. doi:10.1037//0022-3514.52.1.145.

65 Baumeister, R. F., & Vohs, K. D. (2002). The pursuit of meaningfulness in life. In C. R. Snyder & S. J. Lopez (Eds.), Handbook of Positive Psychology (608–618). London: Oxford University Press.

The memory of a child.
How long it has been since I just
watched gazed at a little one
in her mother's arms —
As the flight began, excitement permeated
the 18 month old attention.
She was a "sitter", the term use for
a baby under 24 months that
would remain in her or her mother's
lap for the entire 2.5 hour flight.
Infant in extreme silence would
slowly — a cry or two were quickly
quieted by a bottle of milk.
The mother, conversant, but totally
interested in holding, hugging, kissing
the infant w/ total focus —
A video game, a cell phone
easily — kept the child's attention.
Good spleenness 182